GW00863608

Alice Soule lives in Hertfordshire with her husband Joe, three children, Jude, Elsa and Emmeline and two cats, Patty and Stups. Living with a Jude is her first book built on the back of her blog (of the same name) which follows their family life and in particular the complexities of finding a place in the world for Jude.

A self-proclaimed dreamer, feminist and lover of politics, Alice studied Social Policy at university focusing her work on women's policy and disability in society. Now working as a Content Writer and Author, Alice wants to use her position to express the opinions of families living with a disabled child and in particular to highlight the joys, troubles, hilarities and sometimes mind-boggling scenarios that naturally become apparent.

www.livingwithajude.co.uk

www.facebook.com/livingwithajude

www.twitter.com/livingwithajude

www.instagram.com/livingwithajude

LIVING WITH A JUDE

ALICE SOULE

The Book Guild Ltd

First published in Great Britain in 2017 by
The Book Guild Ltd
9 Priory Business Park
Wistow Road, Kibworth
Leicestershire, LE8 0RX
Freephone: 0800 999 2982
www.bookguild.co.uk
Email: info@bookguild.co.uk
Twitter: @bookguild

Typeset in Minion Pro

Printed and bound in Great Britain by CPI Group (UK) Ltd, Croydon, CR0 4YY

ISBN 978 1912083 954

British Library Cataloguing in Publication Data.
A catalogue record for this book is available from the British Library.

CONTENTS

ACKNOWLEDGMENTS

Thank you to everyone who helped me, either by reading chapter drafts or just listening to me witter on. I know I have an ability to talk! Through blogging I have made some fabulous friends who I speak to every day and who keep me sane when the real world is all becoming too stressful. You know who you are and I thank you all for making me smile and for regularly making me snigger away at some of the fab topics we debate.

Joe. Thanks for encouraging me to write this book, I wouldn't have done it if you hadn't given me that push every now and then.

Love you millions.

Thanks to our stubborn little Emmeline for challenging my patience every day. You truly are the joker of the family but you always manage to shine a ray of light into everyone's life. You are Jude's best friend and I love to watch your relationship evolve.

Elsa. Elsa Pelsa, our little geeky, genius child. You truly are unique, wonderful and stronger than many give you credit for. I'm so sorry you've had to grow up quicker than you possibly would have if Jude had been born your a-typical child but we all have different lives for a reasons. From a very young age you showed yourself as special and I can't wait to see what you make of your life. You have so many talents and gifts and I know you'll use them to your best ability.

And Jude! You should be given a thank you page all of your own because if it wasn't for you I wouldn't be the person I am today. I have a million things I could say to you but will keep it brief. You've brought out my compassion, patience and integrity. You've shown me another world that so many people are blind to but which enriches the soul more than anyone could realise. You've taught me not to care what people think and that there are perhaps a handful of people you can truly trust in life and that embracing good friendships is so important.

Thanks also to my amazing parents for constantly supporting me through life. The amount the children love you can never truly be expressed in words and anyway, I think they show it better in person.

Thank you to all the people at The Book Guild who read my book and truly believing it to have potential. You've been a great support and guide through this whole process.

FOREWORD

This book has been written to show what it can be like to have a disabled child within your family. It is entirely based on experience and I would truly love to hear any opinions people may have on the topics included.

I want to build a community for families like ours so they feel safe to talk about anything and everything affecting their lives. I have never felt supported by any agencies that are apparently available for people in our situation and I thought that if this is how I feel then there will be others like us as well. It's a hard life, a really hard life at times and I want people to read this book and feel they can contact me if they think it may help in some way.

As parents of a special needs child I think it's important to learn from others experiences and stories and I hope our story can give comfort and reflection to those needing something of a sounding board. We are far from perfect. I often think I'm a terrible mother but in reality I know I'm not. I'm just trying to do my best in a situation within which I sometimes truly struggle.

INTRODUCTION

I have tried to think of an analogy that is indicative of raising a learning disabled child but I am struggling profoundly, largely because to me this is normal. Normal. Such a simple but potentially insulting word. So many times, I have heard people describing children around Jude as "normal", so what does that make him? Weird? I guess to many, his behaviours are rather unconventional and even to my autistically trained mind, some of the things he does go beyond his usual quirky capabilities.

I have never really had a chance to breathe since Jude's birth ten years ago. When you have a new baby, it's so draining; the change in lifestyle, no longer really having a chance to think about yourself and just the enormity of having this tiny person reliant on you for literally every passing moment of their life. Every decision and every choice. I was quite young when I had Jude, just turned twenty-five and looking back now, even though I considered myself pretty mature for my age, the whole situation hit me like an iron wall. Not only did I have this brain fog descending over me that you nearly always experience in the first year of your baby's life, I also had to contend with hospital appointments to see the paediatrician, health visitors, physiotherapists, occupational therapists and portage workers, to name but a few. No one ever gave me an indication of what we needed to do to help Jude, no one told me what was available in terms of provisions, support or therapy, I had to literally form this supporting web around Jude, rather like a jigsaw, hoping I was doing the best for him. Occasionally, something wouldn't work out so I would take that piece out, only to replace it with another piece.

But, I like to think I was given Jude for a reason. Potentially a stupid thing to say really but if things always happen for a reason then I must have had a learning disabled child for a particular reason. To say our life is challenging is an understatement but it has taught me so many things that I am grateful for. I accept so much more than I used to, I always look to help people, I notice the specific aspects of humanity and intrinsic behaviours when we're out and about that many would not even see. I think I have become a lot kinder; I'd like to say I'm more patient but genetically I'm doomed in that department as none of my extended family has been blessed with that trait.

Our daughter, Elsa (seven), has said in the past that if Jude didn't have his disabilities then he wouldn't be Jude. That comment has stuck with me for the past three years since she mentioned it randomly at breakfast one day as I think it's a fantastically loving thing to say. Simplistic as only a young child could achieve but also indicative of the acceptance adorning our very young that sadly seems to slowly seep out of our being as we age. Elsa won't admit it but she adores Jude.

There are moments where she lets her guard down and the two of them play magical games in the garden, creating assault courses defined purely by sticks and a few random toys lying about the garden or they drift idly back and forth on their wooden rope swings chatting about things I have never attempted to listen to for fear of breaking that sibling connection merely with my presence. She teaches Jude letters, numbers and tests his addition and subtraction by holding up her fingers and simply asking, "Jude, what's five take away two?" Elsa also, on occasion, helps Jude to fasten buttons, put his shoes on properly and helps him find his bookbag when the bus arrives.

Here is a string of images taken from when Elsa was fifteen months old and Jude would have been three years and two months. I love these pictures; they display sheer innocence, love and acceptance like nothing else can.

But then there is the flip side. Elsa gets incredibly frustrated with Jude and his behaviours and we often forget how important it is for siblings of learning disabled children to have a break from this lifestyle. I need my own time so she must do too. As Elsa grows up, she is going to need more and more of this space so Joe and I have always tried to ensure her bedroom is very much as she would like it, as she needs it to be in order to relax and feel content. It's her own space where she can read her books, write at her desk or just chill out in the peaceful knowledge that Jude won't come into her room; he never really has done and being the creature of habit he is, this pretty much indicates how little interest he has in her possessions or environment in general. Jude can be very full on, talks non-stop and can never seem to walk at a normal, relaxed pace. He's somewhat of a toddler in his motion. For example, waiting at the front door to come in after school, as soon as the passage is free, he will run full pelt rather than walk through to the kitchen and out into the garden. When he realises Elsa is in an irritable mood (pretty often!), he tries to wind her up by copying what she says, poking her, jumping around making silly noises and using all the tools he has that really rile her. This may sound like an entirely typical sibling relationship; however, it isn't. It's magnified an incredible amount plus has the support of all the other stress that goes alongside having a disabled sibling like Jude… the stares when we're out en masse, the constant attention he needs from me leading to her pretty much fending for herself and just the general Jude-ness of our life. Elsa has got to the point where she knows instinctively to look out for him in the manner that I do as his mother! Kind of insane and tragic at the same time for a seven-year-old girl. Or, as stated at the beginning, this is just her normal.

And our other daughter, Emmeline.

She is approaching one and a half years old and we are always commenting on how fascinating it will be to observe her and Jude's relationship as it develops and matures. Already she adores him and I think he adores her too as he follows her around at times and when they aren't together, he asks where she is. They have invented a little game that scares both Joe and me to bits involving jumping on Jude's bed and laughing a lot (I literally have no idea what they find so amusing but I guess that's half of their fun). I hate interrupting it as it's so wonderful to see their connection but I do occasionally have to intervene!

When she was born in July 2015, we wondered how he would react to a new sibling coming home. Despite our best efforts to explain to him that Mummy had a baby in her tummy, because it wasn't tangible or even something he could refer back to in terms of experience, I don't think he had a clue what we were talking about! On day one of her being home from the hospital, he asked a few times when the baby was going home. I kept repeating that, "no, your new sister is staying with us," and in his utter confusion, he asked me "Elsa?". I tried to be as simplistic as I could – "Yes, Elsa is your sister but you have another sister as well now. Emmeline! And she is here to stay." Maybe he did understand, maybe it was more a case of incredulousness... oh no, not another sister!

So, what are the reasons for Jude's disabilities and what exactly is his diagnosis?

Jude was born with microcephaly and global development delay. He is also autistic but this is undiagnosed as I'm bored of hassling the council to complete his assessment. Honestly, you'd think I was asking for everyone in the department to chop off a limb it's been such a painful and dead-end process; I know that's a terrible attitude but I'm going to ask the school to assist me on this one as I clearly can't manage it myself! Initially, the referral for assessment was sent in by the school doctor, however, it seems to have been lost in translation as despite our best efforts, it still hasn't occurred. At first, it really annoyed me because there is a fantastic secondary school that I wanted to look at for Jude, but it is specific to autistic children and without that diagnosis they wouldn't let me even look around the premises. One of the many annoyances of needing a diagnosis! BUT as it happens, there is another fantastic secondary school that Jude will be attending soon so I'm more than happy with this as a substitute.

So, I'm wittering on here but why have I written this book? Well, it has taken me over ten years but I have finally found the strength through my blog and now within this book to face all our issues head-on and I thought it would be pretty cool to initiate a community of families similar to ours that are struggling and who feel very much isolated from the social world and say to them "IT'S OK, WE'LL GET THROUGH ALL THIS TOGETHER!" It can be truly demoralising turning down invitations, seeing friendships wither away because that option is less stressful than attending events and friends' houses and facing the wrath of your child and their possible behaviours. I know this because it has happened to me and I am sincerely really sad at some of the friendships that no longer exist in my life. There are people I have known since childhood yet never see now and I know this is my fault but I can't explain to them why it's happened because they probably won't entirely understand what I am on about. Yes, I know we could just go out and not worry about what people think but it is not that simple. Jude (and children like Jude) are pressure cookers… simmering away beautifully, allowing you the chance to relax and think to yourself, "OK, this is going well, maybe I do just need to go out a bit more often." But then, BAM! Something happens… you may know what it is, you may have predicted it was going to happen (whilst praying it wouldn't) or it may be something entirely invisible to you that has bothered them to the extent they are now lying on the floor freaking out, or crying unreservedly into your lap. Jude can get obsessive with things and it builds and builds until sometimes the situation is unmanageable and I just have to get him home and into his room so he can calm himself down. THIS is the sort of thing you cannot explain to parents of non-disabled children or friends/family in general.

SO, I really hope you enjoy my writing. If not, stop now or else you're going to be seriously bored for the next 111 pages. BUT in all seriousness, this book has been written as a reflection of life with a disabled child, so an awareness and normalisation can be raised that learning disabled people exist, (largely in isolated secret,) in society and to highlight many of the difficulties we face raising these precious children.

I hope you find it helpful – either a comfort of recognition or as a useful incitement into the life of a family with a learning disabled child. Our Jude.

1

CHOOSING JUDE

Accepting into our life the challenge
of a child with disabilities

"A child is only as disabled as their environment and the beliefs of the people around them."

– Bala Pillai DPT, PCS

It's funny really. I've always been very much a coper; I never make a big deal out of situations because I don't like making a scene (how British!) and I'll do whatever is needed to ensure everything runs calmly and smoothly. We attended antenatal groups, involving six couples, with me at twenty-four, being the youngest by quite a long way. During these evening sessions, we discussed the labour and birth at length and touched on life at home with a newborn baby. If I'm honest, looking back, the entire contents of this course were massively different to reality and did nothing for me other than instil a nervousness in my mind that hadn't previously been there. I'm a coper, I just get on with things. Pregnancy/parenthood is a part of life and to me, that wasn't the big deal we were being led to believe it was. Then, on the 20th March 2006, after a horror of a labour, I gave birth to Jude in Addenbrookes Hospital in Cambridge. I had literally just turned twenty-five, was excited and had no feelings that perhaps I was too young or immature for a baby. I was probably very naive but I suppose most first-time parents are, with a brain fogged with confused ideas around the best baby products, notions of how you'll wean, that you'll breastfeed exclusively for a year, suppositions of how your baby will be one of the good sleepers/eaters, and a smiley little thing who rarely cries and grins at every visitor. Does anyone truly consider there may possibly be an abnormality from birth that leads your fluffy cloud of excitement and happiness to reduce itself into a swirling mist of anxiety, confusion and wildly mixed emotions? I know I certainly didn't even entertain this idea.

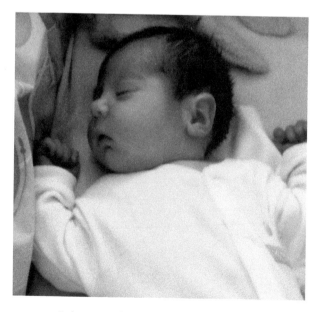

Jude as a newborn, just home from hospital

When Jude was first born there were no indications he had a disability, the hospital staff did not measure his head circumference (or perhaps they did and I didn't realise) so nothing showed up as problematic. As it was, from our first health visitor appointment, Jude's weight and height were perfectly placed on the 75th centile line whilst his head circumference lingered down at around the 5th centile. Not a problem according to the health visitors; they said they'd monitor him regularly and take things as they come.

Jude's first visit to Granny and Grandad's house

I think Jude was merely two months old when I was adamant he wasn't exactly like the other babies in our antenatal group. I would lie him under his baby gym and rather than looking around and moving his arms and legs, he would literally lie there still. It was as if he had absolutely no idea of what was expected of him; there was nothing functioning within his head to tell him to move his limbs or even recognise if someone walked into the room. Over the next few months, I visited our doctor with Jude because of this constant niggling concern that I couldn't get rid of and because his head circumference was not moving off the bottom line of the "normal" range of what it should be, despite his weight and height still remaining on the very healthy 75th centile line. I knew something wasn't right; however, I was repeatedly told that every baby is different and to just let him learn at his own pace or that he's still only very young and that he just needs time. NO HE DOESN'T! Being a mother, you know. You just know and no amount of medical training can supersede the knowledge of a mother! We had our eight-month check a month early and hilariously, Jude passed! From what I could tell, all he had to do was follow a pen with his eyes, show a reaction to his knees and be able to hold something in both his hands. Needless to say, I still wasn't completely happy with this result and after a third GP visit, I was finally allowed to see a paediatrician "just to put my mind at rest".

We saw the paediatrician when Jude was just over ten months old and surprise, surprise, within the first few minutes of our appointment, she agreed that something was wrong with Jude but she wasn't sure what. My feelings at this point were still pretty chilled; we'd get through this and Jude would be fine. Hilariously, I had in my head that we'd work everything out and by the time he would be ready to start school he'd be just like all the other children! What planet was I on?!

Jude at around three months old.

Microcephaly.

I had never heard of it and had barely heard of any disabled children in my arena of actual experience. Surely this was something Jude would get over pretty soon? We were promised nothing, even told that we couldn't be sure when Jude would stop learning altogether, whether he would ever be a "normal" child or whether this would be a lifelong influence on our day-to-day lives. At this point, I honestly and quite insultingly to all disabled people around the world, truly thought that this would be something we would work out and Jude would be able to live the life most children live. All children, no? It's funny really how naive we can be and how we often think certain things would never happen to us. I remember meeting disabled children prior to having my own family as a friend of mine's mother worked at a special-needs school and I never thought I would be like them, like their mothers. That didn't happen to someone like me, surely!? What does that even mean, anyway? I feel so stupid having even thought I was immune to certain aspects of life.

The first thing we did was see a physiotherapist who taught Jude to move from a sitting into a crawling position. Repeat, repeat, repeat. That's what we would do with the motion of moving both of his hands on to the floor to one side of his body so he could naturally learn how to become mobile himself. I remember him getting upset when he didn't want to do it anymore but I was so keen for him to be mobile, be like all the other babies, that I persisted and eventually he cracked it. He crawled on his own and typical for Jude, he did it brilliantly. I don't know what it is with Jude; I think it's a confidence thing that he displayed even as young as toddlerhood. If he suspects he can't do something then he won't even try. Nowadays, it's things like doing up his shoes; won't try and just whinges if I try and make him. Back then it was moving. But again, once he has that confidence, in a split second he's off! Literally as if he's been crawling for months.

Walking was another fiasco. He managed to pull himself up to standing pretty independently but again, was stuck. He just didn't know what to do next so I'd take an ankle in each hand and whilst he held on to the furniture, I'd march him around the room. He'd reach out for tables and chairs and eventually make his way around the house. He was twenty-two months when he took his first steps unaided. Again, it was a long, slow and encouragement-filled process but once he knew he could do it, he literally broke into a run at any given moment.

Jude is still incredibly unstable on his feet and holds on to
the buggy when we're out at the shops.

We then embarked on occupational therapy to help his
fine motor skills, and music therapy because it focused his
concentration and also because he absolutely adored and still
adores music. To be honest, I felt very much as if I was being
led by the professionals as I truly didn't know what we were
doing. I guess no one would as it isn't a situation you ever think
you'll find yourself in and when you do, it's hard to work out

what the best path of action is to take. Think about how hard it is to even make day-to-day decisions for a non-disabled child? Well, you have that plus all the additional stresses of just getting the child functioning at some independent level so they can be understood and can engage in society. Do you go NHS or the private route? Is waiting for the NHS route wasting valuable time or is throwing money at private therapists a waste of finances?

Jude didn't babble or talk as a toddler but the first recognisable vocal communication he displayed was when he was about two and he hummed "Twinkle, Twinkle, Little Star". He could hum most nursery rhymes as a toddler; it was quite remarkable and indicative that his brain could retain information and sounds, hence the music therapy. It was fantastic the support we were offered by Addenbrookes; it often took time but the help was there and we just had to ask for it. I miss all the staff who helped us in Jude's early years. I can honestly say they were all fantastic and without them, Jude would never have progressed as well as he did. This is in part because they were so approachable for me. I felt comfortable enough to ask them questions and ensure I was doing things correctly at home in regard to his movement/fine motor skills.

Jude was born with low muscle tone in all of his limbs and he had massively turned-in feet where he would literally walk on the insides of his feet rather than the soles. We saw specialists who made him little velcro boots that would strap around his feet and hold him in place within his shoes.

In hindsight, my gut instinct that these were not the best idea was probably correct. Instead of helping to build the muscles around his feet and lower leg, all these were doing were holding him in place so a) he was massively uncomfortable and would often get red marks from rubbing and b) the muscles were being held static so were not having the opportunity to develop and gain strength. Surely, it makes more sense to encourage movement and activity in bare feet so as to grow stronger? In fact, after a couple of years, I never took Jude back to have any insoles made and his feet slowly corrected themselves through bare foot physical activity. Now, at the age of nearly eleven, no evidence is left of his wonky ankles except a slight awkwardness in his movement.

Jude was given a Statement of Educational Need at the age of three and this allowed his nursery to part fund someone to be his one-to-one supporter. I was given such fabulous help from Jude's portage worker (play therapist) with regard to the paperwork for this documentation as it was truly baffling; how anyone with a low comprehension level or a disability themselves is able to complete this unaided is beyond me. This lady was amazing and came over to my house one day so we could sit and fill in the pages and pages of details needed for the council to believe he needed additional support. Needless to say, we were awarded the report with no second thought.

Jude had a wonderful time at his nursery – The Wendy House – fantastic staff, some of whom I am still in contact with now. Jude was a favourite with the carers there and in particular one lady, Camilla, kind of became his right-hand (wo)man. She was his one-to-one supporter as it made more sense to use someone he was already familiar with and as he adored her so much, she was a natural choice. I have to say, I was so happy when Jude was at The Wendy House. He was content, so, so content, and I was probably at my least stressed point in life since his birth. The reason he was at nursery was because I decided to return to university when he was eighteen months old and enrolled in a degree in social policy; I would leave for lectures knowing he was in a fantastic place and it was wonderful for me to use my brain again and do something productive that I knew would help Jude and my life in the future.

It was during his nursery years that we learnt some of his quirks. One of his first fascinations was opening and closing doors. Literally opening and closing them! He would work out orders and liked to have certain ones in the house open and others firmly shut and he would hear from any part of the house if one was opened and left out of place which was hilarious – needless to say, the wrongly angled doors would have to be immediately corrected. At nursery, there was a line bordering

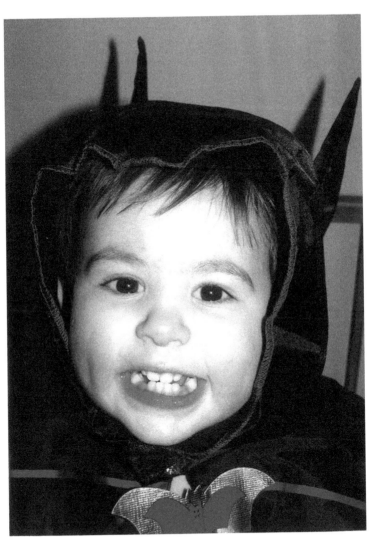

This is one of my favourite pictures of Jude. He was two and a half and
dressed as a bat for Hallowe'en. His smile was beautiful
and attracted lots of attention.

the grass/patio area and he literally would never cross it without holding someone's hand. In fact, he would never cross any lines on the ground and we often joked that to save on babysitters, we could just draw a circle around Jude and know he wouldn't go anywhere! I took him to the opticians following this line discovery. However, they couldn't decipher anything wrong with his vision. Can you imagine trying to test the eyesight of a severely disabled, autistic, barely verbal toddler?! Poor people. Even keeping his head still so they could look into his eyes with the light was a challenge but they checked out his overall eye health the best they could and he seemed fine. He's still now really wary on his feet and won't walk down small graduations on the ground, and it's only recently he would walk down steps without holding on to something. I guess this is down to his poor coordination that was identified early on.

Jude aged four on holiday in the south of France.

Moving back to Hertfordshire when Jude was four was challenging. Firstly, attempting to transfer his Statement from a Cambridgeshire version to a Hertfordshire one which I always assumed would be simple especially as they are neighbouring counties; honestly, the way they behaved, you would think the two counties were thousands of miles apart. I'm not entirely certain of the internal process that occurred in order to change his Statement (or why the change was even necessary... different headed paper?!) but it took a few months from start to finish. Then we moved and I thought it would be plain sailing from then on. We were back in Hertfordshire, an affluent county, so surely provision would be better or at least as good as Cambridgeshire?! Errr, no. Nightmare from day one. Having got used to accessing physiotherapy, occupational therapy, speech therapy, music therapy, any therapy we wanted whenever we wanted in Cambridgeshire, it was a massive shock to the system to be turned down for EVERYTHING in Hertfordshire. So, we couldn't have physiotherapy on the grounds that Jude could walk, we couldn't have occupational therapy because his concentration was too poor, music therapy was not even on the menu, speech therapy – no chance. ARRGHHHH! I obviously fought the decisions but the complexities and networks that you have to navigate in order to just even speak to the correct person were utterly baffling. I have often reflected (and I'm sure I will mention it several times throughout this book) that I feel entirely sorry and bereft of suggestions for the poor parents who have learning disabilities themselves. Attempting to challenge a council's decision or a department within or connected to the council takes a huge amount of time, paperwork and guts. It isn't easy and I'm sorry to say I barely left the starting blocks with my attempt to obtain these fairly typical therapies for Jude. We paid for speech therapy for a short while which was really good and gave me some great ideas as to activities I could attempt with Jude. I think I just wanted the therapist there as much as a support for me as for Jude; just having that other adult in our world who knew people and knew this kind of "thing" because even after a few years, I felt completely lost and numb of ideas as to what I was meant to do with Jude. As it happened, this is generally what most first-time parents feel, however, I didn't realise this at the time and I often wasn't sure what feelings were first-time parent nerves and what was genuine confusion because of his disabilities. I'm a massive over-thinker so this probably didn't help matters either!

The council then did not make the admission into school easy and despite Jude having a Statement that detailed a child with SEVERE learning disabilities, they insisted he join a mainstream setting; this was against my wishes. I was given the chance to appeal the decision; however, it was detailed to me that as it was so close to the summer holidays, we were unlikely to get an answer soon and then we would lose any school place whatsoever until the case was completed. I didn't want to take this risk or have him miss out on any vital education so we placed him in the primary school that I had attended as it was the only one I had had vague experience of… even if this was around twenty-five years ago!

This is Jude on his first day of school. He was so excited and my apprehension was well masked so as not to cause Jude any concern.

I found the year he spent in mainstream very difficult. Many of the parents were incredibly snobby and some would not even acknowledge me in the playground; whether this was to do with Jude or just their supposed social standings, I'm not sure. I already felt horribly nervous and completely out of place so I found drop-off and pick-up times incredibly stressful. Jude made one special friend at this setting and had playdates occasionally with her. However, because of his limited ability to socialise or even understand what anyone was saying, he struggled to make friends. The one saving grace in his reception year was his one-to-one learning support assistants. To begin with, there was one lady but towards the end of the year two ladies shared the role, both of whom he completely adored. We have photos of his time with them and you can see how much they cared for Jude and how much he loved being in their company. The games they played and sensory activities they invented for him were wonderful. For example, one day they re-enacted the book We're Going on a Bear Hunt and took pictures of Jude all around the playground for each page. It's brilliant and despite the book only being about two pages long now, Jude still loves to look at it in bed.

With great joy, Jude joined a special needs school in 2011 for year one and he has been much happier and content ever since. At present, he is in the process of moving to a senior special needs school with an early transfer programme as I just think he's ready and needs a new challenge. Jude can get very complacent if he isn't kept on his toes and the different environment will stimulate him enough and force him to concentrate on his surroundings which is exactly what he needs in life. When things are too easy he becomes lazy! It's very local to us so it'll be nice for us to have a larger part in his school life; I'll be able to drop him off and pick him up each day and thus will meet more parents and be able to speak to his teachers more frequently.

Jude aged six, happy as ever playing in the garden. Jude loves being outside.

I can't really end this chapter without mentioning the addition of my partner Joe, who came into Jude's life when he was six years old.

Joe features later on in this book in the form of an interview but it's important for me to mention him here as he has helped me personally more than he could ever realise which inevitably has had an effect on my ability to parent successfully. I think it's unsurprising to hear that it hasn't been easy for Joe to form a relationship with Jude (even I struggle with that), but he's become the constant in Jude's life that he really needs. I hope for Joe and Jude to bond further; he's like a different child when you take him out on his own so I think I'm going to force more outings for just the boys. Joe and Elsa bonded instantly. I remember their first meeting at the top of an Underground escalator on our way to Winter Wonderland in London; she was shy for a few minutes but then came into her own, going on rides, sharing a pizza and having a fantastic day all together.

We had so much fun. From then on, everything fell into place and she now sees Joe as her father-figure; yelling at him like she does at me, running and jumping into his arms when he returns from work and going on bike rides and picnics to our local woods with no one else invited. She even calls him Doey which is a combination of Daddy and Joey. He was Daddy Doey for a while but is now just Doey. It can't be easy entering into a ready-made family but Joe has undoubtedly been a positive element featuring in the latter part of our first ten years of Jude's life.

Here are the three of us at a wedding in Surrey

So, our first ten years in a very brief outline: it has not so much been a journey of acceptance for myself but more a voyage of self-discovery, of lesson learning and of forming a thick skin. I've always accepted Jude, he's just Jude and for me it's entirely normal to have a disabled child because that is all I've ever known. Would it be different if Jude had been my second or third child? Would I be less accepting having experienced what a "normal" life could feel like?

The two melon lovers watching Elsa, just back from school, eat her slice of melon.

During the ten years, Elsa and Emmeline have been born into our slightly wayward and "different" family but they both love Jude in their own little way, even Elsa who will always vehemently deny it! The girls have each other and Joe and I both revel in how wonderful they are together and how much their mutual love is apparent. Elsa could have become jealous with Emmeline's arrival but in contrast, she has taken her under her wing and sees her as her little protégée; Elsa the Second when it comes to determination and stubbornness! I love watching Emmeline taking in all of Jude. She instinctively runs up to Elsa, knowing the predictable response she will receive of a big, beaming smile, a shriek of joy and a hug followed by a game that they have invented between themselves. Emmeline loves to copy Elsa's gymnastics or she'll just run at her and jump into her arms over and over again. More recently, they have entered the realms of pretend play and in particular Emmeline likes to pretend to feed her favourite cuddly bunny. Elsa knows how to encourage her and they both connect glances in a knowing way, appreciating each other's moves and contributions to their time together. They both accept Jude entirely. They accept him for what he brings to the table and as I'll probably say too many times, they don't know any different. For them it's normal life to have a disabled brother who stops them from participating in certain things because it isn't Jude-friendly and who denies them as many freely encountered playdates as their friends experience. Elsa's relationship with Jude has changed over the years, as she has grown up. At eight years old, she no longer has anything in common with him at all but up until she was perhaps about six, they could still play the silly games that Jude would love to play even now. Hopefully he'll go through that close phase with Emmeline before she, too, bypasses him in terms of maturity. It breaks my heart that he'll never go through what they'll go through but in some ways it may be a blessing. The traumas you encounter during teenage years, adult worries, parental stresses – nothing Jude is going to ever have to contend with. He's always going to be Jude and we accept that, knowing he will always have this childlike naivety, a trust in complete strangers that terrifies me and an inability to ever look after himself.

Obviously in this chapter I haven't gone into entire detail of the past ten years as that would be seriously boring and even our most ardent readers would struggle with the content. However, what I have tried to highlight is that literally since day one it has been a challenge and a responsibility that will be apparent through our whole lives.

2

WHO'S A JUDE?

Autism and its manifestations

"Autists are the ultimate square pegs, and the problem with pounding a square peg into a round hole is not that the hammering is hard work. It's that you're destroying the peg."

– Paul Collins

Oh autism, if you weren't such a serious situation, we would laugh and laugh every day. Or maybe we should be laughing because to be honest, the days I laugh are the ones that pass the happiest. I thought it would be interesting to compile a selection of images that show Jude's autism in its truest form. For Jude, this is primarily through lining everything up. He's obsessed and it never ceases to make me smile! I say "everything" but he does have his favourite objects to line up...

shoes, books, building blocks and inanimate objects found around the garden.

Despite autism (ASD) only being one of Jude's diagnoses, it is the one I am going to focus on because firstly, it manifests itself in such an apparent way whilst microcephaly and global development delay are less obvious. But here is a brief introduction to his other "conditions" (hate that word) – Microcephaly is purely defined as "micro" = small and "cephaly" = brain or head so the easiest way of diagnosing this is through measuring the individual's head circumference. When Jude was born, he was in the normal range of measurements, however, way, way down the chart compared to his weight and height. I think he started on about the 5th centile and slowly slid downwards to zero. Now he's not even on the normal range, however, thankfully for Jude it isn't massively obvious as his sizing isn't as extreme as some people experience.

Global development delay means exactly that– he is delayed in all areas of development. Massively delayed. At his current age of ten I think he functions at around four years of age. There is no telling if this is it and Jude will stay at this level for the rest of his life; no paediatrician would ever make predictions like that and to be honest, that's fine. To a large extent, his development is environmental and dependent on the effort we and people around put in with him but also the effort he puts in himself (minimal!).

SO, autism… everyone has heard of it but do people really know how it shows itself? Obviously EVERYONE IS DIFFERENT and this information below does not by any means define an individual. These are merely indications that people can use if, like me, you are given no professional help in regard to calling a diagnosis.

According to the National Autistic Society (NAS) there are several predictable areas of focus:

Social communication – this is very strong for Jude; his social communication is very, very infantile. NAS highlights the areas of facial expression, tone of voice and jokes or sarcasm as problematic for autistic people and that abstract concepts, i.e. notions you explain to them and expect an element of imagination to be used, are incredibly troublesome. Jude's imagination is awful. It has got better in that he does display some acts of pretend play, however, on the whole, he looks at children as if they are insane if they pretend a random object is a phone or a piece of cake! Of course, many autistic children are non-verbal so communicate through sign language or by usual visual prompt cards. Echolalia is a very pretty name for an incredibly irritating trait that Jude displays all the time at home. It is the act of repeating what someone else has said rather than replying appropriately within a conversational situation. I only recently realised that Jude was copying us because of his disabilities; we assumed he was just trying to annoy everyone (one of his favourite pastimes) – Yes, the guilt has kicked in.

Socially Jude adores going to the park as he is familiar with the surroundings. He always stays on the apparatus he is used to and avoids anything involving climbing as he is so unsure on his feet. This is something I feel really bad about – I should have fought harder for physiotherapy. I should have insisted he needed more support with his gross motor skills but he was always turned down on the grounds that he could walk. As if just being able to walk is enough.

Social interaction – Many autistic people find it hard to function within the social world because of their challenges with understanding other people's emotions and expressions. Jude definitely finds this hard, particularly if we have a group of people round at home; it's as if all the different expressions and intentions are too much for him to compute so he regularly retreats back to his own bedroom for some time alone. And actually, very recently, whilst waiting for Elsa to finish her orchestra practice, Jude asked if we could stand outside because the noise of everyone chattering in the waiting area was bothering him. I was stunned he mentioned it to me as this is typically outside his realms of comprehension but thrilled he felt he could say it to me. Similarly, and I find quite sadly, Jude never looks for comfort as children often do. He never wants a hug or to hold hands, and doesn't have any affection within him at all.

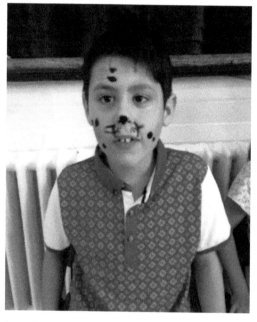

Jude attending a birthday party for the first time since being very young. It was the party of a boy in his class and he had the absolute time of his life. He even had his face painted!

Restrictive behaviour and routines – This is Jude all over! He hates me parking the car the "wrong" way round in the driveway, has to sit at the same place at the dining table, eats the same food off the same plate, plays the same games over and over again, has to have the sun visor CLOSED in the car, has to sit in the same place in the car, has to have everything in the garden in the correct positioning… in fact, for a while last summer, he would have a huge tantrum if anyone even walked out of the back door into the garden for fear we would mess up his patterns! I could go on for days.

Highly-focused interests – This is the only one I'm stuck on as I don't think Jude has any specific interests except playing on his bike or lining up blocks. Perhaps this is because of his microcephaly and global development delay? It could limit his capacity for interest.

Sensory sensitivity – When Jude was a baby and toddler you literally couldn't even touch the palm of his hands because they were so sensitive; he would flinch and pull them away from you. He isn't so bad now; however, he still hesitates before giving you his hand. Jude is very much affected by sound and loves certain things such as swooshing water in the bath. He also loves leaving his bubble tube on at night due to the gentle hum it emits which I think he finds soothing.

We also can't talk about autism without mentioning Temple Grandin. Her work is magnificent and the description she manages to animate through words of a life with autism is simply mindboggling. She regularly refers to visual learning and seeing things purely in images and Jude most definitely has this skill. As a tiny toddler, even before he could walk (he walked at twenty-two months) Jude could remember directions and landmarks that most people would either not even give recognition to or would forget about fairly rapidly. For example,

Jude used to know we were almost home when he saw the trains outside the window on his side of the car. His next indicator would be the level crossing for which he would wait excitedly to move. He knew how to get to his grandparents' house and used to point directions to me merely for fun. He could navigate the corridors of our children's centre and the hospital in which he was born before the age of two. Clearly, he learnt things through images at an early age yet it is only recently that I have given him credit for the knowledge he has.

It's really hard to pinpoint specific autistic traits because ASD is massively diverse and is proving to some specialists increasingly variable in its expression and characteristics. This is probably largely because children with autism often also have other disabilities such as Jude having global development delay and microcephaly. But one thing that is apparent is the massive number of boys in contrast to girls who display ASD symptoms; according to NAS, its schools have a ratio of 1:5 in terms of girl/boy pupils which is quite startling. Why boys? Is this a diagnostic issue as up until recently, the diagnosis for Asperger's was based on characteristics and behaviour patterns of males? Women naturally display characteristics differently and thus are being left behind in terms of support. Some theorists suggest that women are also less likely to be diagnosed with Asperger's because females are generally better in social situations and could potentially mask symptoms more easily. I find this all quite bizarre and am unsure if I buy this second suggestion – I also find it sad that women are potentially not gaining the support they need purely because their behaviours are being analysed on those of males. To have your diagnosis based on a checklist of questions cannot possibly be considered as adequate, especially as social situations can be far reaching and varied in their content.. So, it must be imperative that specialists take each case individually, watch the child, take into consideration influences of friendship circles and realise that girls may copy socially accepted sentences just to be considered within their social gatherings.

I'm not a specialist in any way whatsoever, however, I just relate to people struggling to find an adequate diagnosis. Whilst not wanting to label your child, it's crazily important to have the paperwork, the diagnosis and the reports in order to be considered for social care support. You can't, for example, look around special needs schools without the correct diagnosis. I have missed out on an opportunity for Jude to attend a school I really wanted him to go to because he is yet to have the autistic badge of honour. It's not the school's fault; it is massively popular and obviously needs a set of criteria with which to distinguish its community; however, I am frustrated with the council for ignoring my plea to complete the analysis quickly in order for us to possibly be accepted for a place at this school. I know we can move Jude again but that isn't an ideal scenario; we'll see how he does at his new school in the next few months.

Jude has always loved wheels and ride-on cars. He still does now and can sit and spin wheels or push toy cars back and forth as a way of calming himself for a long time.

So, quite clearly Jude is autistic! There are so many examples I could give of times his autism has got the better of him (or us). For example, regularly when in the car and it is sunny I'll put the sun visor down. Perfectly normal, you may think. NOT WITH A JUDE – you can literally see him getting twitchy the moment my hand moves towards the visor so I'll just look at him and say, "Jude, it's OK." Predictably, he'll ask if I'm putting it down soon... then he'll ask again and again and again until I either give up and replace the sun visor thus risking blindness or Jude puts his visor down too so it looks symmetrical! Just for amusement (because truly you need to sometimes) I'll wind my window down slightly. Again, Jude's twitchiness begins so he'll wind his window down to exactly the same height. Without looking at Jude, I'll alter mine slightly and as soon as he hears the window move, he amends his window's height too! This can go on for entire car journeys; it's insane! Even Jude thinks it's insane because he always laughs along with me.

Another way his autism comes out is with Jude's hearing; it is incredible. Saying that, his talent is very selective because I'm pretty sure I have to ask him at least twenty times to come downstairs if I want to talk to him or because we are going out somewhere and I need him to get his shoes on. But, in general, his hearing is amazingly acute in terms of hearing background sounds or music amongst a foray of other sounds. We can be watching television, or the radio can be on in the kitchen but if my phone rings and it's located in my handbag in the hallway, he will hear it and tell me. Or he will hear someone walking up the driveway before anyone else. In a busy room, if someone starts gently singing a song to themselves, he'll join in and I'll have to really listen to see who he is copying.

One of Jude's longest running habits is regarding glasses; as in reading glasses/sunglasses, etc. I'm not even sure this is autism related, it's just really odd! Basically, if he sees a pair of glasses lying on the table, he has to hide them. It's like he can't stand seeing them, they literally offend his eyes (ironic). He has been known in the past to take a pair of glasses, go out into the garden and throw them in hedges. Or he'll put them down the back of a drawer in the kitchen or worse still, in the bin. He knows he's not allowed to do any of this any more so if my glasses are in the kitchen and he happens to notice them evilly looking at him, he'll build a little wall around them using jars, tubs, anything lying around so that he can no longer see them! It's hilarious! My dad has a slightly mean (but again very funny) trick of taking his glasses off and asking Jude if he'd like to wear them. Again, Jude finds this funny so he'll laugh and say no thank you.

It's funny because despite all of this, I don't see Jude's traits as because of his autism, I just see them as an element of his character. He makes annoying noises, sometimes flaps his hands and squeals excitedly and this doesn't scream out "autism" to me; it's just Jude.

Then there is the pièce de résistance – Jude's lining-up habit. This can only be described visually so here you go…

3

REJECTING A JUDE

Society and isolation

"Keep your face always toward the sunshine – and shadows will fall behind you."

– Walt Whitman

My first experience of negativity in society happened before Jude was even eleven months old and before he had even had a diagnosis. We used to attend a playgroup near to our house which even in the early stages I was wary of because of the understandable habit many parents pick up in this environment of asking if your child can hold a spoon yet, or if they can pull themselves up to standing, or have they said a word yet, etc. For the first year of Jude's life I dreaded this and my flustering blurted out made up explanations as to why Jude had only just sat up at seven months (actually not that bad), and hadn't tried to stand or grab something yet. Why do we feel we need to justify our experiences to relative strangers? Maybe it's just me; in fact, I know it's largely about me as back then I was always very wary of how I looked to other people. Maybe it was an age thing – at twenty-five, I was still very shy and hated confrontation. So to take Jude to a playgroup when I knew he was a bit different was quite a big deal to me. Thankfully it wasn't massively obvious at this age and he still looked like the cute little baby that everyone expects; he was able to function relatively to age as, let's be honest... you can pretty much fool people into believing they can do anything at this age: "Oh yes, at home he literally feeds himself an entire bowl of porridge and he's only eleven months old!"; "He ran from one end of the room to the other this week, I don't know why he's being so silly today", etc. I'm sure we've all done it. Justified our child's behaviour to someone we don't even know so they look as they should to society.

Jude was merely a toddler when we began experiencing negativity. Here is Jude aged two years and ten months old with his new little sister, Elsa.

Anyway, back to playgroup at eleven months old. I was speaking to a friend of mine about the paediatrician appointment we had been to a couple of days prior and I was relaying what she had told us, that there was definitely something not quite right with Jude and that he would need to see a physiotherapist to get him moving a bit and all of a sudden, from about five metres away, a woman I barely knew to even say hello to said, "Well, what do you expect him to do at his age, run?" To say I was gobsmacked is an understatement. I literally wanted to cry. Here I was, fearful that something was definitely wrong with my baby and this woman was judging me and my expectations. Stupidly, and I can't quite believe how much I have changed since then, I tried to explain myself… "Well, I was told to see the paediatrician by my GP. There's definitely something wrong with him," I babbled away. SHUT UP ALICE, IT'S NO ONE'S BUSINESS!

Jude showing off his nine millionth crisp of the day. He was taking advantage of the fact we had guests to make sure he sneaked as much food as he could into his mouth!

So, isolation begins from the day you find out your child has a disability. You suddenly don't feel quite so accepted in society, you don't feel like you have the same experiences or the same options in life for you or your child. Here we were, trying to work out how best to help my disabled child and already what Jude should or shouldn't be able to do was being flung on his shoulders by a stranger. Now, I know she didn't say this knowing there was anything fundamentally wrong with him and I'm sure many people do see paediatricians for a consultation and nothing occurs from this but that isn't for anyone else to judge.

Ever since Jude was little, I think I have gradually changed as an individual; I know most people do but it is definitely from living with a Jude that has enabled me to become what I now feel I am. I have gone from being a shy, justifying, people-pleasing doormat to a much stronger, questioning and thick-skinned woman thanks to the many experiences we have had from the outside world. I say outside world because honestly, I don't feel like we belong entirely to the real world sometimes. Even the thought of simple day-to-day tasks like walking into town to visit the market makes me shiver and automatically many, many possibilities of why this could be a nightmare pop into my head. We wanted to go and visit a French market not long ago but Jude flat-out refused to leave the house, had a huge tantrum when I made him put his shoes on and ended up screaming, lying on the driveway until I caved in and let him go back up to his room. What can you do? He's a strong boy now, I can't frogmarch him like I used to. Thankfully for us, my mum was able to come and sit with him so we could at least escape the house for an hour or so as a "normal" family. Jude regularly doesn't want to leave the house at weekends. I don't know if it's laziness or that he's just getting worse with his routines and wanting to control his environment but I'm not entirely sure how we can progress from here. I don't think Jude is aware of being different to most people. I hope he isn't, it would be horrendous to contemplate how sad he would feel if he began to see the way he behaves compared to his peers.

When younger, Jude was such a happy child and adored our day trip to Peppa Pig World (aged three and a half).

A more recent experience where I literally wanted the ground to swallow me up was during a summer holiday trip to the swing park. For the whole walk into town, Jude kept reminding me that he wanted an ice cream from the ice-cream van and I kept reiterating that we would get one AFTER we played in the park. I could sense him getting more and more wound up and panicked as we slowly gained distance and he was asking me more frequently with every step! On entering the walkway up to the park, Jude completely lost it and had a full-on autistic melt-down on the floor. So, here's the scene – big treelined pathway, me pushing an empty buggy, a newly liberated toddler legging it around in circles and Jude, lying on the floor screaming. Ho hum, another fun outing. People walking past varied from ignoring us, having a glance and a frown, giving me a consolatory half smile to full on staring. A small group of teenagers walked past and one of the girls nudged her friend, pointed and laughed. I could feel the rage building in me and truthfully, if Emmeline hadn't chosen that moment to run off in the opposite direction then I would have said something to her. What a cow. I could have cried but I went in to autistic parent survival mode and somehow managed to get Emmeline in the buggy, Jude on his feet and slowly walking back towards the entrance of the park so we could creep the mile home again. Many people have asked why I didn't just give Jude the ice cream to start with and this is an obviously understandable suggestion that only parents of non-disabled children would offer. When Jude is in this mood, nothing will help. If I had got him the ice cream he would have just thrown it and had another meltdown; it's pretty much a lose-lose situation all round. The best thing to do (for us anyway) is to get home and find Jude his safe space which is traditionally his bedroom. Phew. But that experience will haunt me for a long time as I felt like a goldfish in a bowl. I know what some people were thinking as I've had people come up to me and say it before: "Why don't you try and listen to him?"; "Perhaps he's tired."; "Oh dear, did he not get what he wants?"; "We can't always get it our own way.".

BRILLIANT. Thanks, people! The best comment I've ever had was in a posh supermarket when Jude was about five years old. He was having a random tantrum and I was just leaving him to it as there was literally nothing I could do to make the situation better and an elderly lady came over and stood watching for a few seconds. I was about to ask her why she was staring at my son when she came out with the cracker of, "Perhaps he just needs some love." I'll leave you guys to mull that one over…

Following our hell in the swing park I wrote a blog post that has, even to this day, been my most read article. I wrote it whilst still very emotional and despite my best efforts to contain this,

I think it comes through still pretty strongly. I posted it on our town's Facebook page and it sparked over a hundred remarks and likes. This is it:

For all the good days we have had this summer holiday, it was inevitable that things would only deteriorate as Jude got more and more frustrated with our chilled-out routines each day. He loves school. He needs the_structure and stimulation that he gets from the virtually constant one-to-one set-up he has there and I obviously can't give this to him at home because of the girls.

So, today... oh today, what a day.

Things started badly but this has been a pattern for the last, maybe five days, so it didn't surprise me. I like to take Emmeline for a walk so she'll have a nice nap plus we can get out in the sunshine for a while at the same time. My dad came over to join us this morning *and* had suggested we go to a cafe in town that we love but even before he arrived, I'd had an inkling we wouldn't make it that far. We didn't. Jude flat-out refused to move off the driveway, lying on the floor for extra effect. Anyway, ten minutes of trying to convince him failed and we ended up back at home, him screaming in his room but Dad, myself and Emmeline out in the garden to make the most of the sunshine. There is absolutely no point in talking to him in this mood, so I just leave him to it upstairs.

He's bored. I know he's bored._But there is only so much I can do at the moment with zero funds and frankly, an ever decreasing level of energy for this summer holidays.

This afternoon, I thought he was in a more reasonable mood so promised to go for ice creams by the park. It started out fine, we went and fed the ducks, Jude and Emmeline ran across the Common together and then we walked into town so I could get some money out for ice creams. I said (about 900 times) that we would go to the park first and get ice cream on the way home.

Emmeline loves running up and down hills at the moment and Jude found it hilarious trying to coax her in the right direction (3rd picture).

But then it went horribly wrong in a way only a parent of a disabled child would understand. Jude started getting more and more anxious about the impending treat and repeated over and over again that we were going to the ice-cream van. I tried to remind him that we were going to the park first but by then it was too late and he completely lost it at the entrance of the park. He screamed and cried like a two-year-old, shouted at me whilst flapping his arms and everybody stared. I just stood there not knowing what the best plan of action was. Parents of disabled children have coping mechanisms for every possible eventuality and it's just a matter of working out which one best suits the scenario you find yourself in.

What made this experience worse was a small group of

young teenagers who thought it OK to laugh at Jude._Yes, amazing but true. Not all four of them laughed, just one girl laughed. She_then looked at her friend_who_too laughed on command of raised eyebrow. This is my nightmare. I'm in a big park, I have the buggy with Emmeline in and I somehow have to get Jude back to his safe space at home. I've no idea how I managed it but eventually, after much walking off by me and even more screaming on the floor by Jude, metre by metre we made the mile-walk home.

This is Jude in all his glory, crying on the floor.

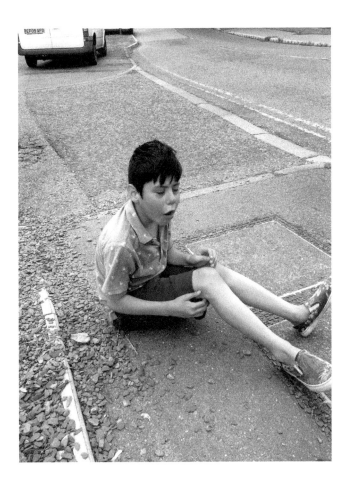

It's rather ironic that this happened today because following a fabulous trip to the park yesterday, I was going to write about how absolutely lovely a pair of teenage boys had been towards us. Jude wanted to go on a swing so one gave up his place for Jude to have a go. He even agreed to push him! Then when Jude said he wanted to go on the big swing (big, round swing that seats a few people) and I said we'd go on when there were fewer people there, the teenager said to me "I'm sure they'll move up a bit for him if he wants a go too."

It was such an inspiring visit; I almost felt like a valid member of the swing-park community at that moment.

But back to today... what a spectacle. I felt like a freak show. And following such a day...

I have one request – if you see a child who clearly has learning disabilities and they are throwing a tantrum, please don't stare at them. It's a certainty the parent already feels awful enough and could literally jump off a cliff at that given moment. Just help by educating your children that not everyone is the same and that some children speak differently, walk differently, play differently, act differently but everyone is as important as each other.

I'm really drained from today. I was feeling confident about all things Jude and it's amazing how quickly that bubble can be burst into a million drops of stress and anxiety.

Another recent supermarket experience involved a lady with her two children aged about eight to ten staring full on at Jude as he did one of his funny little movements. Nothing spectacular; I think he was holding on to the trolley but jumping around its perimeter so I just carried on choosing carrots but I could see this family in the corner of my eye. I thought the lady would have had more sense but clearly not and the three of them carried on watching Jude who danced away in oblivion. I could feel the anger rising again so stared back at them until I caught the lady's eye and asked her what they were looking at. She said nothing but hurried her children away clearly aware that she had been caught staring. Now, I know many people do not do this with malice or negative intention but imagine going out and constantly being stared at, commented on, pointed and laughed at. It hurts and it makes you feel like a lesser being in society. Thankfully, Jude isn't the bearer of these emotions, it is just me.

We took the children to a festival this summer and Jude managed to cope with it for a few hours before we had to leave. He did well because it was pretty noisy, there were a lot of people around and there was the potential for him to become massively overstimulated. He did eventually but it was great to be able to take him somewhere a bit different for once.

Thankfully also, not everyone sees us as the town entertainment. Shortly after the starey supermarket experience, we went to a local art supply shop to buy a birthday present for Elsa's friend. I had to leave Jude for a few minutes as we were in a rush and I just wanted to pick something and get out. Literally a few minutes later I could hear Jude chatting to someone. Oh no, I thought, because half the time people ignore him and you never quite know who he is picking as the victim of his typical questions. Phew, it was a lovely lady and truly, scenarios like this fill my heart with joy. I walked around the corner to see them both sitting together having a chat. They looked a hilarious sight: there was a smiling Jude, happy he had found someone to chat to and next to him was a tattooed, pink-haired woman smiling and looking directly back at Jude. I so wish I had taken a photograph. When Jude is in this situation he rolls out his favourite questions... Where are you going? What are you doing? Next time, do you want to come for lunch? (He saves this for door knockers at home!) Is your car hot? (He has to touch every car he walks past.) Are you going now? But this lady just answered and reciprocated with questions of her own. Jude looked like he could burst with excitement!

Anyway, so there we have it. This is why so many people with disabled children choose to remain within the confinements of their safety. It's very Russian roulette when you go out... in its most simplistic form, will you meet the good or the bad? Is it worth risking going out somewhere that will be highly populated because you know you will all be stared at and if you are tired or drained, this can make it feel a million times worse? Holidays are a whole other ball game and to be honest, from now on we are probably not going to take Jude away very often because it's stressful for us and stressful for him. It negates the whole point of a holiday! He doesn't enjoy it, the elements of change are too frequent and profound for him to cope with so we end up spending each day just making sure Jude feels comfortable and this largely means remaining in our hotel room. My parents and I took him and Elsa to the US a few years ago to visit friends and I think I lost a few stone in stress just thinking about the flights there and back. We coped fine but I had to toughen myself up in preparation for the potential situations and as an autistic child's mother we have every scenario banked away in our minds with recovery and survival techniques optioned away just in case.

Jude on holiday in the south of France aged three and a half. He was a lot more flexible when younger, coped well with change and in participating with day trips on holiday.

I could write for hours about how isolating it can be with a disabled child and this is without even touching on the subject of financial isolation that many parents experience in this arena.

It's a startlingly scary fact that four in ten disabled children live in poverty. That's a huge amount. But for me, living with a disabled child, I can wholeheartedly understand how people end up in poverty (or never manage to get out of it). But before I offer my suggestions as to why, here are some statistics found on the Joseph Rowntree Foundation website.

1. 28% of people in poverty are disabled and this includes 310,000 children.
2. An extra 20% of people in poverty LIVE in a household with a disabled person.
3. 25% of working-aged disabled people have an income of less than 50% of the national median income.
4. Disabled people face higher costs of living than non-disabled people with 18% of working-aged disabled people being unable to even afford basic items due to costs.

Honestly, this breaks my heart. What angers me the most is the demonisation of disability that much of the media has created within this country. When you think of someone as being on disability benefit, you would be forgiven for instantly having negative feelings about this thanks to many programmes and newspaper articles attempting to disprove their disability and thus indirectly labelling them as lazy and "spongers". Love that word – sponger. Is Jude a sponger? Yes, he has use of his arms and legs and could technically work when he's older but what if mentally and emotionally it's too much for him? Not all disability is visible and there is much written on hidden disabilities that is not as readily displayed as articles denouncing large portions of our dependence in society as villains.

Why do we chastise the people who need our help the most? The government is making changes to the way in which disabled people are given support and it appears to be purely to the detriment. Here is an example... not directly relevant for Jude but just go with it and have a think...

The government has a scheme, "Motability", that allows disabled people to lease mobility scooters, cars and electric wheelchairs thus enabling those with a physical disability to display an element of independence. BUT our current government has changed the rules which has led to up to five hundred people every week having to return their vehicles because they are no longer eligible. Part of the, rather insulting in my opinion, test to prove whether you truly need one of these products used to be to show you cannot physically walk fifty metres unaided (enforced via the Department for Work and Pensions). The government has changed this distance to twenty metres (yes, just twenty) and thus dramatically reduced the amount of people able to lease directly through them. It's believed that over 30,000 had to return their vehicles, their lifeline to independence, by the end of 2016. How sad is this? Why do we not just help our disabled people and the families who live with them? I just find it all so sad.

So, back to my theories on poverty. Why are so many children literally living on the breadline when they already have the hardship of disability to face day to day. Well, I have two main trains of thought, neither of which I really considered until Jude went to school:

1. Disabled parents. If a child has a disability and it's genetically formed, the chances are that one or both of the parents will have a disability themselves and will therefore find themselves either unable to find work or in poorly paid roles themselves. Some of Jude's friends' parents have disabilities and I honestly do not know how they cope. Hats off to them, literally.

2. Issues around childcare. I have always tried to find jobs that are term-time only. I even qualified as a teacher so I could work around my children (well, Jude) because I have absolutely no idea what I would do with him during the end-of-term holidays, let alone the long summer break. Elsa and even Emmeline could go to summer camps, spend time at a childminder's or with a nanny but Jude… where does he go? I know there are summer camps specifically for disabled children but they tend to be shorter hours and there is no way in the world he could cope in one of the standard groups. Plus, he'd need someone

I am lucky that I am able to take up part-time employment because my mother, very wonderfully, looks after the children for me as and when necessary. The children have an amazing relationship with their granny and look forward to spending time with her. I literally couldn't cope without her practical support and both Joe and I are eternally grateful that she allows us to function at some normal level.

one to one with him all the time and I doubt any group leaders would forfeit a member of staff purely for Jude. So, what jobs can you do that fit around the school schedule? Very few people are fortunate enough to be able to dictate their own hours unless they are self-employed or work from home during the holidays so this naturally leads to one parent (if there are two in the house) staying at home and revoking their employed status. This obviously leads to less income. If you are a single parent then it is even harder as you may end up having to survive on state handouts and forever displaying your invisible badge labelling you a sponger! I joke… sorry, not funny. But this is how you are often made to feel! And how frustrating for the parent, fully able to take on a career but unable to leave their child in anyone else's care.

I can vouch for this frustration. I have seen job advertisements that I would literally kill to apply for but the thought of finding after school and during holiday childcare is a nightmare. We employed a nanny for a short while when I returned to teaching earlier this year, however, Jude did not cope at all well and I was left entirely stressed every morning, wondering what he was up to as I drove down the motorway. We thus decided that spending so much of our hard-earned money just so I could engage my brain really didn't add up and I left barely before I began. I hate to mess people around, however, I needed to prioritise my family and everyone's well-being so sadly, my career had to be put at the bottom of the priority list.

So, isolation is something you can experience both physically but also emotionally because of the disparity of working experiences, salaries as well as cognitive and career-oriented expanse. Isolation as a parent of a disabled child is a massively deep subject and I promise myself I will research it fully and write extensively on this at some point in the near future.

4

A FRIEND FOR A JUDE

Socialisation and friendships

"The world worries about disability more than disabled people do."

– Warwick Davis

Friendships in childhood can be a massively complex and confusing situation as it is, let alone when it involves a Jude! Jude wants to socialise and have friends but he struggles with what to do with them and how to function when they are nearby. A couple of years ago, he went through a bad phase of hitting and, obviously, the thought of him seeing friends during this time was a big no-no, but now he is out the other side and I know he would absolutely love to have friends over more often, or at least meet up for a playdate. Do you ever see disabled children socialising together in society? I know I never have which is sad but I can totally understand why.

Let's give a few scenarios – firstly, geography. Jude's school has people attending from towns all around it. Some of his friends' parents do not drive, some have disabilities themselves so taking his friend out would involve me collecting them all and I just don't have the room in my car for this. Regardless of the geography, if we invite a friend over this will involve not only looking after my children but there will be a second severely disabled child in the mix unless I invite the parents over too and then it's just a whole busy nightmare in our fairly small house! I did speak to one of Jude's best friends' mothers just prior to the summer holidays and we mentioned meeting up at a park, however, it never happened and I do not have her phone number to initiate the date. This all sounds rather pathetic, I know; however, when you are rushed off your feet with day-to-day life, time goes past and you find yourselves struggling to fit it all in especially when you are just relieved to get through the day unscathed. I have made a vow to suggest an outing with a couple of classmates via Jude's school contact book (teacher-parent contact book in which I can ask for messages to be passed on to various parents) over the next few weeks. I think it would do Jude no end of wonder for both his confidence and understanding of the world. He would love to meet up with some of his peers and it would be amazing to witness his response. Would he play WITH them or would they just say hello and run off and do their own thing? It would be fascinating.

We recently employed a very part-time support worker through council funding as, firstly, a respite option for us but also as a way of Jude experiencing the social world without the aid of his mother or stepfather for company. Not cool when you're nearly eleven years old. I can't get excited, we only have ninety-five hours a year but this equates to a few hours a fortnight for him. Sadly, his first support worker left her position to spend a year abroad teaching. However, within their time together they had some fantastic fun including trips to a crazy golf centre and a bowling alley. Jude had an awesome time and he always referred to her as his friend because that's what we told him she was. Obviously, he wouldn't understand the concept of a support worker so we just introduced her as his friend and that she wanted to take Jude out sometimes to have fun. Realistically, it's the best way for Jude to attempt to crack his way into the social world and to be accepted by others because, with us, I just think it's too close to home. With a support worker, the time together is solely about Jude and they can focus on enjoying themselves and teaching Jude how to conduct himself in an acceptable way. Yes, I know we don't need other people's acceptance but when you have disabilities and you aren't generally accepted by many, it must feel amazing to just experience "normal" civilisation occasionally and if this involves behaving in a particular manner then I don't think it's a bad thing.

It's pretty sad when you're at a play centre or soft play area and Elsa runs off and makes friends without a second thought, however, Jude is always left on his own. I need to start thinking through his mindset because actually, even though playing on his own, he's still really happy. Saying that, there has been the odd occasion when children played with Jude and you can see his whole personality change; it's quite remarkable. It hasn't happened so much recently because ten-year-old boys don't play in a way that appeals to Jude and obviously younger children just see him as a big kid. He's tall and ungainly in his movement so even the bravest four and five-year-olds would keep their distance from engaging in any social activities with him. A few years ago, he and Elsa made friends at a soft play centre near us and despite the fact he wasn't entirely sure what they were doing, he loved running alongside the children, jumping in the ball pond and whizzing down the slide on mats with his new best mates and his sister. It was fabulous to see and is one of the most positive experiences we've had when out and about.

Jude and Elsa play together at a soft play centre. They are both pretty much too old for this environment now but we were really there for Emmeline. It stunned me and made me so happy to see the two of them run off and play together for over an hour. I didn't have to watch out for Jude or make sure he wasn't doing anything he shouldn't be doing. He played like a normal, non-disabled little boy and it was just incredibly warming and beautiful for me to experience a trip to a play centre in a way that most people experience it with every visit.

Another that is lodged in my mind happened not long ago at the park (yes, we go there a lot). Jude wanted to go on a swing and very loudly asked me when the boys on there would be getting off (two teenagers of about thirteen). One of them heard him and immediately said, "Here you go, mate, you can have it," and he hopped off, holding the swing still so Jude could clumsily park his backside down. Moments like this make my heart melt with acceptance. Whilst they engaged no more with Jude, the mere fact that they treated him like a human being made me so humbled and emotional. There are some truly lovely people out there and I feel bad I didn't say anything more than thank you to this young man as I doubt he realised quite how much he really did in that one small action.

Jude and Elsa participating in a clay spinning activity. Jude needed a huge amount of support and thankfully the lady understood and really gave him her undivided attention. He didn't like the feel of the clay so gave up pretty quickly but I was proud that he had put himself in this situation.

The best experience of socialisation Jude has had recently was at a school friend's birthday party (see image of Jude as a dog in chapter 2!!). Needless to say, I, Little Miss Optimistic, was dreading it. I was taking all three children and was unsure as to how Jude would cope in a hall full of people he largely didn't know (and none of whom I knew), lots of running around and a disco bouncy castle which I actually now think is a brilliant invention. It's basically an enclosed bouncy castle with flashing lights and music playing inside which means the children get to go crazy inside and you aren't deafened by it on the outside. Win-win! I have never, ever seen Jude have so much fun. It was amazing. He and Elsa ran off together to play and it got to the stage where I felt so confident that he was safe, content and had been accepted by everyone that I didn't feel the need to watch him so intently. He and Elsa spent the whole two hours together and Jude even sat to have his face painted! It was wonderful! I guess being the party of a disabled child, there was never any fear of Jude's behaviour being considered strange so I relaxed and because the room contained his school friends, he felt like a "normal" functioning ten-year-old. One boy that he adores walked past and Jude even said "Hello, Daniel" off his own back. I was so excited! We had attended a party en masse and it had gone brilliantly! I felt like a normal mother for once! This experience has inspired me to arrange a birthday party for Jude in March as I think he would really love it. In fact, he mentioned that he'd like a birthday party; just something small but special for him to remember. He's never had a party before and I think it would indicate a massive step forward in his socialisation.

I read so much about isolation and the loneliness you experience when living with a disabled child and I can wholeheartedly agree with everyone's thoughts. It isn't just Jude's socialisation which has decreased, it's all of ours. Elsa cannot have friends over so readily, especially if Jude is going through a bad phase like he was not so long ago. It coincided with being pregnant with Emmeline so I was exhausted enough without inviting further children into our home for playdates. Thankfully, he is going through a better patch and when Elsa has friends to play he generally leaves them to it as he knows Elsa doesn't want him to join in. I don't think this has anything to do with his disabilities/strange mannerisms, I think it's just because he's her brother. Being an only child I can only go on what other people have told me but most say that they never wanted their siblings to muscle in with their friends; they were over to play with them and the sibling just had to go and entertain themselves. Obviously, this isn't particularly kind-hearted and perhaps I should be encouraging her to include her brother in their games but, for now, I allow Elsa this space as it's nice for her to have "normal" childhood experiences as often as possible; friends over and playdates are one small luxury I want her to have. I feel eternally sorry for and guilty towards Elsa not being able to experience many things that her friends do as routine and I think this is why I give her a break any time she's rude and overcompensate by ensuring she attends all the activities and lessons she wants to, which is a lot. She's incredibly talented and intelligent which helps in some ways as we've been able to discuss Jude's disabilities and she understands why I often say no to playdates, why I can't take her to the theatre, why we have to cancel that trip to the shops at the last minute, why we can't walk to the park because all of a sudden Jude has decided he won't leave his room. And each time, she is fantastic and doesn't make a fuss. It amazes me the patience and love she shows towards Jude, playing games with him that she knows he enjoys and giving him the chance to win when she knows she could wipe the floor with him (and for someone as competitive as Elsa, this must really be difficult). OK, she isn't all sweetness and light and on many occasions when Jude wants to play she says no, shouts at him and tells him to go away but then which siblings don't speak like that to each other? Overall, Elsa is Jude's best friend and when she's a little older I will discuss with her about her upbringing and how she made my life so much easier than it would have been if she hadn't come along.

She is more than my best friend, she is my lifesaver. So many times, she has read my thoughts and supported me in a way no young child should ever have to do but I think with having a disabled brother, life is always going to take a slightly different route to the norm.

Jude and Elsa then aged nine and six.

At their favourite cafe drinking smoothies.

Elsa and me at a wedding when she was two.

Elsa as a three-year-old. Even at this age, she was more mature than most, taking on responsibilities not many three-year-olds have to and learning independence far more rapidly than I would have ideally liked her too but it was necessary as I often had to tend to Jude.

Jude and Emmeline have recently begun playing together which is something we have anticipated as Emmeline moves into her toddler years. They love spending time together on the hammock swing in his room as well as bouncing on his bed together (it literally gives me a heart attack but I don't want to deter them as he is just so happy). Jude and Elsa used to play similar games but as she has grown up, overtaken and now moved way away from Jude cognitively, he prefers to play with Emmeline. She adores him, sees him as just her brother and enjoys his company a great deal.

How relaxing does this look? Jude pushing
Emmeline gently on his hammock swing.

Jude and Emmeline chilling out together on the couch.

So, we're back on the playdates again, but what about me? Well, I rarely invite people over during the day if Jude is at home probably more out of habit than necessity these days. When Jude was younger, it was hard to sit down and hold meaningful conversations with anyone as I'd have to be up and about tending to Jude so often; making sure he wasn't doing something unhelpful in one of the other rooms, not eating the entire contents of the fridge, escaping out of the side gate or front door, not emptying everything from my make up bag, drawing on walls or ripping up books. The list of possibilities is endless! He doesn't do this now and actually, unless he's in one of his funny, hyperactive or overly emotional moods, I probably could invite a friend over for a bit. It's potentially a bit ridiculous but I would only invite people in whose company Jude is happy so as to keep the peace. He adores some of my friends so I really should make more of an effort. Rather pathetically, I have lost a lot of friends over the years and for this, I'm desperately sad. It was hard to explain at the time how I felt but I needed to face this alone and because I didn't have the typical baby/toddler/child experience most new parents do, I didn't feel I could inflict us on to other people. I remember visiting one of my oldest and closest school friends for a weekend and even though I was so excited to see them, I was completely dreading it. Jude was a hyperactive toddler at the time, touching everything, running around and bleeding me dry of energy from all his crazy behaviour. I had zero confidence and just felt like we were the freak show everywhere we went. I think that was one of the last times I have been to stay overnight at someone's house with Jude. How awful is that? I'd love to visit family and friends who are dotted all over the country but there's no way I'd take Jude for fear he freaks out. Just thinking about it, I can visualise a whole host of nightmarish situations unfolding involving tantrums, freak outs, solo dances in the middle of a restaurant… eeeekkkkk! It isn't happening. But as such, it means Jude misses out. We all do! I don't care so much about myself missing out but for Jude it's important. We're lucky in that my parents are a massively focal part of the family and regularly take Elsa to parties or out for day trips. Elsa even had an overnight stay in Paris with her granny a few months ago. How wonderful is that?! She had the best time ever so I'm eternally grateful to the social support they offer Elsa.

Elsa and her granny are fantastically close and she confidently strode off towards the Eurostar train with her wheelie suitcase behind her. My dad dropped them at the train station and he said how wonderful it was to see them both happy in each other's company.

I need to be braver. So what if Jude talks to literally every person in the restaurant?! He's happy. Or if he does dance or sing one of his favourite songs really loudly and everyone stares? Why do I care so much about the thoughts of a stranger!? I need to focus on Jude's wants and needs and thus initiate that playdate and invite those friends around. Come on, Alice, use that thick skin you've been honing for over ten years!

I've always been keen for Jude to develop some interests that could possibly turn into out-of-school activities but there isn't a huge amount that he enjoys. Jude loves swimming and is now confident enough in the water without any armbands or a noodle; he achieved his twenty-five-metre badge in year five and was incredibly proud of himself. Using our ninety-five (part) funded hours, we could enrol Jude in a whole manner of activity groups but I've read the options at least thirty times and nothing jumps out at me as very Jude-friendly. Multisports? No, he doesn't "get" sport/Craft clubs – not a chance. Any team-based activity – Jude doesn't understand the whole notion of competitiveness and I think he'd drive his teammates mad. Basically, I looked at every option and the best for us was just to use them on his support worker. I think this is the best outcome for the whole family because we need these Jude-free hours as much as he needs stimulation and to be honest, the thought of driving to another extra-curricular activity and waiting round for him really doesn't appeal. I need to be utilitarian in my thinking regarding these hours and the best outcome for the largest amount of people here is Jude going out one to one and we having a bit of respite.

BUT, back to hobbies… there are a few forest school clubs around here so I may try and register Jude with one of them as he loves the outdoors. However, we then have the dilemma as to whether Jude would need a one-to-one supporter (yes), in which case I'd then either have to stay myself (errrr, no thanks) or employ a support worker to support him during the activities… this sounds expensive. Our main success seems to be with individualistic experiences, so Jude went horse riding with the Riding for the Disabled organisation when he was about five years old and loved it! Sadly for us, Jude had a bad reaction to possibly the hay and every time we went, on our departure following the lesson his breathing would be raspy and he'd have a rash on his face. Needless to say, we stopped the sessions. BUT as with many young allergies, Jude is now fine with horses and attends riding sessions through school.

One other activity I initiated for Jude is yoga. The relaxation support as well as the strength it builds, the heightened body awareness and physical coordination make it an activity I just knew would be amazing for Jude. Other benefits of yoga for children can include learning body confidence and forging a positive view of the self and it can encourage and develop concentration. Children are taught a way of managing stress and anxiety through breathing techniques, meditation and exercise that can be completed without any guidance or apparatus. It's also lovely to feel part of a positive community and yoga really does feel like a community when participation is regular.

So, after a few conversations, a wonderful lady from the Special Yoga Foundation based in north London came out to do an initial session with Jude one to one but unfortunately, he completely freaked out and refused to join in. He was definitely listening to what we were doing (whilst flitting from room to room) and I'm certain that if we'd carried on for a few hours he would have better engaged. However, the money cost as well as the fact Jude reacted so negatively put me off continuing on a one-to-one basis. I think Jude sees home as his relaxing space where he can follow his little rituals and habits, and to have this "work" forced upon him, even in the most incredibly unpushy, engaging and exciting way, was all too much for him. Their centre in north London is quite a way away, however, I think I'd like to try and take Jude up for a group session at weekends so we can spend a bit of time together, just Jude and Mummy, which really never happens any more. Especially with cling-bags Emmeline! So yes, that's it really. Despite the fact there are now many, many activity groups specifically for disabled children, most still are very unsuitable for Jude. I guess it's just a matter of trial and error and I should be pleased that I've found a couple of options for him to try and pursue and this will hopefully bring out the social bunny in him. We'll see :)

5

FEEDING A JUDE

Food and nutrition

"Real food doesn't have ingredients, real food is ingredients."
– Jamie Oliver

FOOD! Jude's favourite thing in the whole world. I often revel in the fact he literally has hollow legs and he has most definitely inherited my greediness. What does he like best? Fruit; he loves any and all fruit. In fact, all three children are proper little fruit bats. He also loves pasta, just plain or with a bit of pesto. Beans. I've talked about his bean obsession in my blog and it continues on now… beans in any form: green beans; kidney beans; butter beans. He could just have a huge plate of beans and would be as happy as a pig in mud. What else? Cereal. Jude can get massively obsessive about cereal so there have been times where I have put a blanket ban on cereal even being in the house (I'll explain why in a minute) but yes, if he could have about twenty bowls of cereal a day then that would suit him perfectly. Any cereal, as long as he can shovel it in with a spoon whilst watching Swashbuckle on TV.

So, why did I ban cereal? It isn't the only food I have banned at times. Biscuits, crisps, chocolate, fruit juice. This is all because of his ability to become so entirely obsessed with something that it takes over his life and sends him into a crazy tantrum if he can't have them. He literally turns demonic and it builds up and up to a point where he then throws the food if I eventually cave in and give him a third or fourth helping. There have been times where I have woken up to the screeching of a dining chair being pushed across the floor and I've scurried down to see Jude literally hanging out of the cupboard looking for the biscuits that I've hidden. Or there were the few weeks (months maybe?!) that Jude would get up way before everyone else and raid the fridge. I'd find entire punnets of blueberries gone, whole packets of sweets, he'd hide bags of raisins and chocolate in his room and I'd find the wrappers later that day. If I put some leftovers in the fridge for lunch and Jude got there before me then he'd eat them whatever the time and without thought of what they may have been for. It literally drove me mad. I got to the point where I almost bought locks for the cupboards and the fridge but I didn't because I desperately didn't want to turn our house into a confusing environment for Elsa. I know she understands about Jude and his disabilities but I'm very aware that she is growing up and needs her home to be as typical as possible. I avoid using the word "normal" but that is pretty much what I mean. I've always wanted to make Elsa's, and now Emmeline's as well, upbringing as similar to their friends as possible. Jude inflicts a lot on our immediate family and I'm aware of how stressful at times it must be for his siblings.

I'm lucky in that Jude, Elsa (and now Emmeline) all adore fruit.

I have considered getting Jude's thyroid tested but backed away from it for now; we went for the initial blood tests about two years ago and Jude cried and panicked so much that the nurse took the needle out prematurely when she had only saved a small amount of blood and predictably, I received a letter saying we needed to go back to collect an adequate sample. No thank you! I know it's his health and a few minutes of confusion and unhappiness is menial in comparison, however, he really freaked out and even I, the normally ice queen of emotions, hated it too. We'll do it once he's moved schools and perhaps get their opinion first.

I just wonder whether Jude is genuinely hungry all the time or whether he isn't capable of understanding what it feels like to be full up or if perhaps it is to do with his thyroid.

One thing that bothers me is the amount of poor quality, processed food you see disabled children eating at special needs schools. I put it down to lack of understanding plus the fact many parents are disabled themselves or on the poverty line (or both). I remember being at Jude's school when I stood as a parent governor for a year and at lunch, I was truly horrified by what a lot of the children were eating. Now, I know I'm a health freak and not everyone cares quite to the same level (i.e. they're normal) but some of the packed lunches were entirely made up of packaged foods which are devoid of many nutrients and valuable energy needed by young, growing bodies. Now many children can cope with this, however, when your child already has challenges in life you really need to help them progress and grow as strong as possible so their brain works to its maximum capacity and they stay healthy. I know Jude is prone to stomach-related problems (he was hospitalised three times as a baby/toddler with gastroenteritis) so I make sure the food he eats is clean, digestible, full of fibre and nutrients and gives him plenty of energy. Now, I don't mean for this to sound like a "well done, Alice" praise whilst I sit here and polish my halo. What I really want to focus on is the fact that many disabled children are not eating very well. Families on the breadline can't afford lots of fruit and healthy snacks. They buy the bare minimum necessary and with the lack of education families are given on nutrition, it is no surprise they opt for the less healthy, more convenience items. I won't go into one of my rants about food, however… I always encourage people to buy products that are both inexpensive and nutritious such as grains, beans and lentils for good bulky soups and stews and whilst I know Joe will laugh at this one, another food to always have in stock is my old favourite; porridge oats! I'm always hungry and the only breakfast food that has ever filled me up is porridge so I eat it habitually every morning. A big bag of oats is cheap, filling and delicious if made with milk and a few slices of banana and a sprinkle of cinnamon and sugar. Buying lots of frozen vegetables is also a great way to ensure nothing goes to waste; we always have some mixed vegetables, peas and sweetcorn in our freezer but you can literally buy any vegetable frozen.

I don't want to elaborate too much on specific foods but if you're interested then I often write about nutrition and food on my blog :)

A treat for Jude and Grandad and no one else!

Have you heard of the autism diet? Sounds pretty simple but only if both parents are on board. Sadly for us, Jude's father will not fully entertain even an attempt at this diet despite the fact it MAY prove positive for the wee man. Basically, it involves eliminating all gluten and casein from his diet – two proteins that have proven hard to digest for some people. This, for us, isn't massively challenging because the children eat barely any dairy as it is (casein is a dairy protein) and finding gluten-free products is pretty easy these days as you can get gluten-free anything now from supermarkets as well as specialist shops. For those unaware, gluten is the protein found in wheat, barley, some oat brands and rye. Foods that many gluten-free-ers typically had to avoid such as bread and pasta can now all be purchased gluten-free-style so, like I said, it isn't a massive deal. The problem I find is explaining to Jude why he can eat some bread but not, for example, the bread at Granny's house if he wants a snack; it would involve me being super organised which doesn't come naturally to me!

So why specifically gluten and casein? Well, I'm going to confess to not possessing a single scientific gene in my body, however, according to the charity Coeliac UK, there are two theories as to why removing these proteins could help ASD behaviours.

Firstly, they consider that perhaps excessive levels of peptides from casein and gluten contribute to the typical behaviours displayed with ASD. It is thought that because these peptide levels are evident in urine samples, it has proven too hard to break down during digestion. These peptides may be active biologically and because small amounts cross over in the brain, it can interfere with neurotransmission (i.e. messages to and from the brain) and this can disrupt activity and sensory experience.

Theory two – this is based on enzyme activity that has been altered within the liver. It is thought that this can stop the protein from absorbing within the gastrointestinal tract and therefore again, have an impact on the central nervous system by way of seeping through the large pores of the gut.

Because of these suggestions and because it relates to literally everything a child attempts to digest, for the GFCF diet to possibly stand a chance it needs to be taken on full-pelt. Therefore, for us, I find it frustrating that every fortnight our efforts may be destroyed. However, I do intend to send his father details of the diet in an attempt at one last chance to give it a go. BUT I want to make it clear that this diet should only be considered if you have spoken to a nutritionist first because eliminating foods from the diet of a child is always a big decision especially as so many ASD children are fuss-bags when it comes to food anyway. As I mentioned before, Jude adores pasta but at least this means I can just buy gluten-free instead. It's definitely worth speaking to professionals first as I would hate for people to inadvertently upset their child's body by removing things they may struggle to replace. Dairy-free milks are in abundance in all supermarkets and we buy several different ones each week

– soya milk, oat milk and hemp seed milk are regulars in our fridge as are dairy-free cheeses and yoghurts. As I said, it is a big change in diet if you don't already avoid certain things like we do, so please, please speak to someone first and plan your meals in advance so you don't panic and lose nutrients.

So, one thing I'm particularly intrigued about is what would count as the diet working? What effects can you witness?

Some people have suggested that the autistic traits that sometimes seem to fog an individual's entire being are lessened, that they appear clearer of mind and thought. Others have noticed a level of calmness about their child, better communication, eye contact and general socialisation; less of the anxiety-ridden behaviours such as biting their own arms, screeching and having tantrums when things aren't as they want, and children appear more responsive to questions and requests from parents. Basically, it sounds somewhat miraculous in some cases, however, we must be mindful that these are the extreme cases and actually, if you look at cold, hard science, the GFCF diet is not proven. I would argue that this is perhaps because not enough money is put into trials, however, we can only speculate. In reality, I think parents of ASD children would try anything once, just to gain a bit more of a thought pattern recognisable to the social world within their child's head. I know I would do anything to give Jude a part of my brain to fill the sections missing within his but as I can't, I need to try other things. This I will try but only with guidance from a nutritionist and as long as his father tows the line…

In the meantime, continuing talk of Jude and his beloved food… he has a packed lunch at school and because he finds sandwiches boring, I always attempt to create him inspiring lunches that are varied and (obviously) healthy! Here are some examples of what he has had recently:

You know me, I'm a health freak at heart but occasionally cave in and put a biscuit or cupcake in his packed lunch. Needless to say, this goes down very well.

6

TEACHING A JUDE

School, education and beyond

"The job of an educator is to teach students to see the vitality in themselves."

– Joseph Campbell

I feel rather disenchanted with Jude's education at the moment. I think I'm having a bit of an internal battle as to what the purpose of school really is when you have severe learning disabilities; I don't mean, what is the point in it, I just struggle with what I want Jude to get out of the experience. I was really frustrated at the end of last term when I heard that Jude's class had been learning about Florence Nightingale – come on, honestly?!?! Jude needs to learn how to look after himself, how to dress himself properly and how to make a sandwich. At present, Jude cannot do up buttons or zips so why do we not focus on these basics until they're mastered then move on to other self-help lessons and finally, once he is able to survive entirely independently, we can learn about significant historical figures. Jude loves school and he particularly loves maths lessons. He can do simple addition and subtraction and can match number symbols to their quantities. He has also recently mastered writing his name but struggles with all the other letters without literally tracing over them. He recognises nearly every letter of the alphabet and because of this we have regularly considered purchasing a laptop for him so he can quickly collate his thoughts in words and not have to worry about forming the letters manually but I'm just not sure; I have a fear Lazy Jude would come out and he'd no longer practise his handwriting if he knew there was another option!

Outside of these basics, at school he does a lot of sensory work, physical activities, music lessons and recently began horse riding. This is all fab but I really think they should be paralleling this work which he loves with lessons dedicated to self-help skills. I imagine once he begins secondary school, they will attempt a lot more life lessons such as how to use money, how to make a cup of tea, etc. I hope. I'll ensure this happens. I've learnt a lot from his schooling and feel that I've let weeks, months and academic years pass without keeping on top of exactly what Jude has been doing at school. I know life is busy for everyone but I have a weight of guilt sitting on my shoulders about this. I know no one is perfect but I intend to be a lot more zealous in my contribution to Jude's educational planning once he moves schools later this term.

One of the highlights of Jude's school experience is his journey there and back. Because the school isn't nearby, the council offers transport in the form of a taxi that goes and collects the children from each specific area. There are around four children on Jude's route and they always collect the children in the same order.

This is Pete, Jude's long-standing and beloved taxi driver.

Pete has helped so much in Jude's education in that he has made the drive to school and home again so much fun that he actually looks forward to it each day. They listen to music on the radio and have even christened each day of the week a special name just to make everything that bit more interesting. The council changed taxi firms a couple of years ago and Pete's replacement was horrendous. Not only was the vehicle completely unsafe – think Transit but with metal-legged seats roughly stuck in – but the driver and the escort had not one clue as to how to look after disabled children. The van could barely make it up the hill and was so loud I could hear it chugging around the corner without even having to open any windows or the front door. It was disgusting! The icing on the cake was when I heard the "bus" arriving so went to wait for them by the front door. As there were a lot of cars parked near to our driveway, rather than parking up safely next to the curb the driver merely stopped in the middle of the road and the escort slid the door open for Jude to jump out. Yes, she let him jump out in the middle of the road and run from the road to the front door. I was horrified. I complained and after a short while, Pete was returned to us. Hooray! Things like this are a nightmare and cause Jude no end of stress. When Pete goes on one of his many holidays (lucky man), I always dread who his temporary replacement will be. We've had people unable to grasp the fact that we need to know what time they'll be arriving as some parents have to go to work, i.e. don't turn up forty minutes late without a forward phone call to warn me. It was incredible. Jude was getting more and more worked up and I was freaking out about how I would get Elsa and Jude to school in different towns at the same time plus get to work myself in a third town. Nightmare. Anyway, we muddle through those times but it's worth it because Pete is just so fabulous for Jude. We will really miss him when we move to the new school...

Jude's current school was purpose built specifically for the children around five years ago. It's a fantastic building with beautiful gardens and playgrounds around the back.

Jude adores school, he has friends as I've said before, but he really doesn't know how to interact and his relationships are largely dependent on his mood at the time. For example, he went through a fabulous phase of actually trying to speak to his peers, working alongside them well and generally socialising in his own little way which usually involves playing physical games of jumping, rolling around or just running (!), saying hello and wandering around together, sometimes singing or clapping hands. But one day this week, he decided to shout at his friends instead and he managed to aggravate one boy to the point where he bit Jude on the arm. This is how unpredictable Jude can be and why many people are probably massively put off from being his friend. Jude came home that afternoon, wailing about being bitten by this child (the teachers can't explicitly tell you who was involved but Jude always lets me know anyway) but to be honest, I try to explain to him that if you're going to wind people up to that extent, what do you expect?! He does it for a reaction and when he gets it he displays a strange sense of achievement. But he's also surprised and sounds quite hurt at the same time. When he was explaining what happened during "Bite-gate" he put on a mock upset, whiney voice, like he knew that's how he should sound under these circumstances which is actually really sad. He clearly copies Elsa which is good in a way I suppose, however, I also find it incredibly sad that Jude possibly doesn't feel he can just be himself.

Anyway, school… so, for me, I really just want Jude to learn how to interact, how to look after himself in terms of cooking, dressing and general self-care with a little bit of basic maths and literacy and art thrown in. At the moment, for Jude, he really doesn't need history lessons. I'm sure some of the pupils enjoy it and have the capacity to understand the lessons and abstract concepts but actually this is one of the great things about most special needs schools – they personalise and adapt the curriculum so well. So, for Jude at almost eleven, he is more than likely doing work that is rather different to the rest of his peers in the classroom; it'll basically be personalised. None of the children has "typical" neurological development like in your standard UK classroom so it isn't feasible to do whole class lessons for the bulk of the day.

Jude standing ready for the bus.
He gets anxious if it's late or he thinks he may not be ready in time.

Jude is so proud that he can write his name legibly now.

Jude is almost eleven now and I'd be lying if I didn't express an element of concern as to what he will do when he hits sixteen and is possibly no longer at school. I'm also concerned as to where he may be with his emotional state and with his behaviour, social skills, independence and confidence. Will he still be able to live with us? I desperately hope he calms down and learns to express himself more positively as he travels through the teenage years as otherwise, I'm not entirely sure how we will cope with him at home unless we have a more full-time support worker in tow. I actually would love this for him once he's a teenager anyway, as it will allow him the socialisation that he needs plus he will learn so much from the one-to-one time and through going about day-to-day tasks with what is fundamentally a personal tutor/ friend/companion/supporter and ally.

So, children are expected to remain in education until they are eighteen, however, after sixteen this does not have to be at school. Options are as follows:

- attend college
- work-based learning course
- employment
- voluntary work
- receive support from social services or local children's services

I did read that these options are subject to council provision so based on recent experience that doesn't fill my heart with optimism! What can Jude do? I know this sounds very defeatist but I cannot even muster a vague image of Jude at college, in employment or attending a course through work-based means. Voluntary work!? Perhaps. And the final option is what I dread...

More positively, I read that if local colleges cannot offer a suitable form of education for your child then socialist colleges further afield can be a possibility. This would obviously involve residential stays and again… will our council fund this? I guess they would have to if nothing local is adequate and to be honest, I struggle to see what would suit him beneficially.

Saying all this, here are some good organisations that help disabled people post-sixteen and I guess over the next few years I need to start searching out the ones I think he would enjoy the most, the ones he can benefit from and where I generally think he would like to be. Earthworks (http://www. earthworksstalbans.co.uk) is a beautiful place I have visited a few times that allows disabled adults to grow vegetables, fruit, herbs and learn woodwork and crafts eventually creating objects to sell at the monthly farmers' market in town; they even sell home-made apple juice. I've always loved the outdoors and especially allotment space so I think this is why Earthworks appeals to me so much; similarly, Jude loves being outdoors so it should cover off a few of his interests. I'm hoping that he can join there at sixteen as it would keep his brain active and give his work a great purpose, making a bit of money as well through the monthly market stall.

Jude loves being outside and until he started morphing into the lazybones he's recently become, we used to go for lovely walks across to the woods near our house. He enjoys playing in the fresh air and just wandering around taking in the world around him. This could suggest that future college courses and work focusing on the outdoors may suit Jude's needs.

To be honest, without seeing into the future and knowing what Jude will be like in another six years, I'm not entirely certain what disabled adults do with their time if they aren't able to attend college or get a job, so I thought it would be interesting to speak to some parents with older disabled children to find out what their plans are post-sixteen for their children. Here are some of the quotes:

One parent whose son (diagnosed as autistic) is doing well academically but struggles with learning in a typical classroom style said that he will finish secondary school and go on to agricultural college as he wants to work in that industry and following that he will move on to a degree. She said because she and her partner understand his potential, they are not letting him take an easy route out of education. This is fantastic to encourage him to aim high! Not everyone learns by staring at books in a room full of people so I guess it's trying to find the best way for your child to thrive. Another parent who has a severely disabled child is rather unsure of her son's future. He is now fifteen years old, cannot write or communicate clearly and she fears for what he will be able to do once school finishes in a year or so. She is beginning to look out for activity clubs, social scenarios and support networks that will be able to keep his mind active and stimulated as, otherwise, he can become quite hyper and disruptive and following full-time schooling, he really can't suddenly have a huge void in each day of his life. He has a family-funded support worker twice a week but this will need to be increased once school is over.

Another parent said that their daughter (who has autism) attends mainstream school at present with support and will be moving into the sixth form next September. Following this, she is very unsure but possibly (hopefully) employment of some sort or college if she can think of something in which she is particularly interested. At present, she is just grateful for every day her daughter will physically go to school as she is struggling with certain teaching staff, any change of routine and just life as a teenager.

One lady wrote a very sad reply in regard to her son's education. At present, he attends a school for severe learning disabled children and has been at this school since he was four. He is now sixteen. She hopes he can attend a specialist college when he reaches eighteen, however, because this is out of county she will need to apply for funding and this for her is daunting and soul-destroying. I think she is exhausted from raising her son entirely herself for his whole life and has not gained a great deal of willing support from their local authority. She sounded like her whole life since having her son had been a battle. I can completely understand this. And the exhaustion. Life is exhausting; working out what to do next, what is best, where funding will come from, which department to speak to, who needs to write the next report, etc. Draining.

Finally, a lady whose son has Asperger's – when he was younger he attended a special needs school that has links to a local mainstream school and then he moved to a specialist college at sixteen where fantastic skills such as glass blowing and basket weaving are taught. At nineteen, he was meant to move into assisted living, however, the specialists didn't feel he was ready so he continued on in college and chose to study towards an accountancy-based course. He did really well but couldn't quite complete it because of the necessity to attain a certain amount of hours of work experience. It's a tragedy that this now twenty-eight-year-old man does not have anything functional in his life, he does not work and does not have any friends because he struggles so much to be around people. What makes it even more tragic is that the council is not helping a great deal and on many days, he struggles to even get out of bed and get dressed.

THIS is my fear: Jude becoming this lost individual who is neglected by the council and does not have the abilities or skills to support himself either financially or in terms of care. I have heard of many great specialist colleges around the country, most of which are boarding or at least part boarding in structure. When Jude begins secondary school, I'll be sure to look at all possibilities as I think something like these formal post-sixteen educational establishments may be best for Jude. It will extend his learning and hopefully with maturity behind him he will find something he likes to do.

So there we have it, not massively conclusive but at least I have clarified that I really do not know what Jude will be doing once he completes his education. Excellent!

7

WHAT A JUDE LOVES

Weirdies, favourite things and fascinations

"If we are to achieve a richer culture, we must weave one in which each diverse human gift will find a fitting place."
– Margaret Mead

So, a while ago, I wrote down a list of all of Jude's funny traits that I renamed his "Weirdies". I don't mean funny as in laughing at Jude; what I mean is the traits he displays that are endearing and unique, the ones that make me smile as well as the ones that even Jude has a laugh at!

I wanted to write them down as I knew that once we moved on to a new obsession, I would probably forget some of the more intriguing ones from years gone by… this was my list from the summer time:

When he gets out the car, he won't shut the door himself

claiming he can't do so but the minute you start walking towards him, he shuts the door with a bang.

If you open a window in the car then Jude has to open his to exactly the same level. Ditto the sun visor!

He needs a plate to eat ice lollies.

Before he goes to sleep, he likes to play with building blocks in bed. He lines them up according to colour and then moves them round in some strange little code only Jude understands.

Jude won't wear socks. Ever.

I parked the car facing the house rather than reversing into the driveway a while ago and it freaked him out. All evening, he kept going to the window to look at the car in a kind of "I need to make this OK" situation. I went and turned the car back the "right" way just so he could lie down and sleep.

Glasses must be hidden at all times – as in the reading glasses/sunglasses variety. He can't stand them and if he finds a rogue pair accidentally left unattended, he'll either put them in the bin, hide them behind jars or whatever he can see on the table or he has also been known to shove them as far back in our top (junk) drawer as possible.

So, I have a few additions to this list… obviously, we have the lining up of literally anything, which has definitely become more elaborate over time.

Jude is obsessed with lifts, he knows where all the lifts are in town and regularly asks if we can go and see them. He can also make lift doors out of anything.

"Dooooors opening," he recites as he moves the lift doors back so he can push the passenger through. "Dooors closing," as he shuts the doors so the lift can get going. And repeat.

Parking. As in parking his car, go-kart, my office chair, anything with wheels basically! He lined up a few books by my desk recently and told me he was just going to park the car; he then proceeded to shuffle his feet so the office chair crept across the floor and fitted snugly in the "parking space" he had made.

This parking fascination is displayed everywhere but most certainly began its life in the garden:

He also has this strange fascination with making things wobble. A few years ago, we used to find shoes precariously balanced on door handles (no, I'm not kidding). I remember watching him do it once and the concentration on his face was incredible. He would place the shoe on its side along the length of the door handle and then move it forward slightly so it wasn't resting against the door but being held up entirely by the handle. He'd watch it for a few minutes as the shoe gained its equilibrium and once still, he'd move on to the next shoe! Anyway, this wobbling fascination has continued and he does amusing things such as holding a plate with two hands flat underneath and then walking with a slight skip to his feet so the plate moves around. Needless to say, he sometimes accidentally flicks a bit of food or a fork or knife off his plate which he simply finds hilarious!

He's always loved pushing things around and up until we insisted on my mother chucking it away, Jude used to spend hours walking around their garden pushing a manky old buggy. Following on with the balancing/wobbling fascination, he would often balance a little plastic shopping trolley, a bike helmet, garden toys, whatever he could find on the top of this buggy and then carry on walking around the garden watching it all move. My dad used to say he looked like a little Steptoe and he did with all his treasures on his buggy! Thankfully the buggy has long since been ditched but if given the chance, he'll push anything he can around the garden. When he was about five, Jude used to push chairs around our house and the scratchy noise against the floor used to drive me MAD. I'd find dining chairs in the hallway balanced with one leg up on the front door; he'd always leave his chairs at precarious angles. It was honestly like walking into a joke house at times!

Another wobbly/balancing thing was his obsession with his police car. You know the little plastic cars that children sit in and propel themselves along with their feet? Well, up until early this year when Jude was about to turn ten, he could STILL fit inside his car! He'd shuffle around the garden, no idea how, but he would somehow contort his body so he could fit his bandy arms and legs inside. Again, we had to get rid of the car or else Jude would still be playing in it now. Elsa used to wind him up and when he was inside, she'd go and lie across the top. Jude would freak out and try to swat her away with an arm out of the window. It was pretty funny to watch. How awful is that? Obviously, I'd stop her eventually but you have to laugh sometimes…

And that's the thing with Jude's obsessions. They don't go away unless you make them. For example, you have to throw things away because otherwise his play becomes deconstructive and actually it ends up detrimental to his learning. He can be so fixated on something that nothing else in the entire world matters. If someone touches that thing then he explodes. It may seem mean taking away his favourite thing but every time we've done this, he has quickly moved on to the next stim. Because that's what it is, really. He's not playing like any other child would play; it's simply fulfilling a need. Probably like a drug addict needing a hit, Jude needs to line things up, or feel the bumps on the ground through his car or flick bits of paper around so as to calm his mind. Did I just compare my son to a drug taker? Whoops.

Finally, water. Oh wow, does Jude like water. He can sit with a paddling pool full of water and sieve it, pour it, stir it or just watch the water move. It's been a bit of a long-term fascination and one that has reared up again recently with Jude filling buckets and buckets of water from the bathroom to pour slowly down the plughole. He just watches the movement. It's amazing to watch his eyes and wonder what he sees as the water trickles away. His eyes change when he's in a stimming mood – they almost glaze over with wonder. He's not observing what he's doing as you or I may do, so I wonder if it's merely the sensation he needs; the feel, the sound, just the general experience. I find it so interesting. He also wants to have a bath every day at the moment (impressive for a nearing-teenage-life boy) but it's not because he wants to be clean, it's because he wants to flick water. Oh yes, Jude can't just sit in the bath and wash himself. He'll crouch on his feet, look down and swipe his hand across his body, just touching the water so it flicks, over and over again in a repetitive motion. The sound is really irritating for me (welcome to his world, I guess!), the water constantly hitting the side of the bath in a swift, swishing splash.

I have read recently about how many people (not just children) with autism are massively attracted to water but amusingly, another connection Jude and trillions of other autistic children seem to have is an overly enthusiastic obsession with automatic doors. Jude can tell you, like the lifts, where all the automatic doors are in town. In fact, he often asks if we can go and see them. He can stand in front of a set of doors, wait for them to close and then run across the front, not quite touching them but just near enough so as to set them off. He then runs back to exactly the same spot. If someone interrupts his game to use the doors as they were invented for then he patiently waits for them to close once more and off he goes again! If you look up autism and automatic doors there are literally hundreds of articles citing the same fascination! I have been reading quite a lot on why children with ASD like things such as water and automatic doors and my main conclusion is that they think through a series of images and these images or sounds or colours fulfil a need for that child and by doing so, anxiety is kept at bay, balance is maintained within their internal environment and everything is OK. The world is broken up into pictures according to Dr Temple Grandin, a fantastic writer on all this autism. Honestly, read some of her essays or books as they are essential for any parent of a child with ASD. This quote below really hit home and gave me something to think about.

Children with less severe auditory sensitivity problems may be attracted to sound and visual stimuli that more severely impaired children tend to avoid. I liked the sound of flowing water and enjoyed pouring water back and forth between orange juice cans... I liked the visual stimulation of watching automatic sliding doors; whereas another child might run and scream when he or she sees an automatic sliding door... When I look at moving sliding doors, I get the same pleasurable feeling that used to occur when I engaged in rocking or other stereotypical autistic behaviors.

Quote from *My Experiences with Visual Thinking Sensory Problems and Communication Difficulties* by Temple Grandin, Ph.D.

This is Jude! Jude doesn't seem to have severe auditory sensitivity as he never covers his ears or seems afraid of loud or low, consistent noises so perhaps his need to play with water is because of the sound. Similarly, with vision, Jude doesn't seem anxiously bothered by many things but is incredibly attracted to bright lights such as his bubble tube, the disco ball attached to his bedroom curtain rail or the colours of the television. In fact, this is probably why he likes to sit where he does every day. Jude never sits, he crouches on his feet in a way I can only sustain for a few minutes. Jude can crouch on his feet, like a little owl, for literally AGES.

He does this just to the side of the TV so he can see the colours of the screen at the top of his eyeline, thus covering two stims and obsessions in one go: the lift game (doooors opening!) and the attraction of light (from the TV). It's just all so amazing really and quite pronounced how more and more autistic he is becoming as he gets older. Is this even possible? Probably not, but it's just how it appears to us at home. By researching more about his needs and by observing him frequently I'll be able to understand his own little world and hopefully crack my way into it occasionally.

8

OUR THOUGHTS ON LIVING WITH A JUDE

Musings of a sister, step-dad and Jude himself

As is typical of me and because I think each chapter concluded fairly succinctly, I'm going to do something a bit random in this chapter. I'm going to interview my family to gather their thoughts on Jude; what he's like as a brother/stepson, what the expectations are for his future, etc. so here we go... starting with Elsa.

Me: So Elsa, what is Jude like as a brother? Is he fun?

Elsa: Annoying, but funny as well. He's annoying because he takes all my stuff from my room and just screeches and shouts at me for no reason. He's funny because sometimes he lets me in his room to play with him. I like jumping on the bed with him and playing on his swing.

Me: What are Jude's best characteristics?

Elsa: That would have to be... long pause... happy and joyful and he can be quite kind.

Me: What annoys you about him?

Elsa: Comes in and takes my stuff away from my room and says they're his but actually they're mine. Such as he takes my animal toys (Elsa collects mini models of animals) and he kept taking my skateboard and playing with it and then he said it was his and hid it in his room so everyone thought it was his.

Me: Is there anything you'd change about Jude?

Elsa: No. He's him.

Me: What do you think Jude would be like if he didn't have disabilities? Do you think he'd like different things?

Elsa: I think he wouldn't be all like "ah nah nah nah, this is mine" and I think he'd let me on his swing more and be a bit more friendly. I think he'd like to do things like lots of races with me. I don't know really.

Me: What do you think he'll do when he's older? Will he work and live on his own?

Elsa: I think he'll live with someone. No, I think he'll just work in a company or sell houses or cars, definitely cars because he loves cars. I think he'll live alone but people will visit him more often; like you (me!) will see him more, and me and Emmeline and Joe and his friends. He'll need help but people will just come to visit him socially.

Me: Any other thoughts on Jude?

Elsa: No. Actually, yeah, he could not make such a big mess in his room, that would be good.

I find it heart-warming and so insightful into the mind of a child that Elsa truly believes Jude could live on his own and hold down a typical daily job. In the eyes of a child, people are just who they are; there is nothing "wrong" with anyone. Ever since she was a really little girl, Elsa has always maintained that she would never change anything about her brother. That's just who he is and deep down she would defend him to the death.

It's humbling and in some ways shameful that as adults we attempt to change people and mould them into something they are not, just because our crazy, fast-paced and expectational society deems that we must comply. Why should we? Jude's just fine how he is. Elsa is proud of her brother and doesn't give two hoots what people stare at when we're out and about. I need to follow her lead more; she's a very wise soul in an eight-year-old's body.

Next up is Joe – my wonderful partner, father to Emmeline and (step)dad to Elsa and Jude.

Me: Joe, where do we begin? Jude. Give me your thoughts…

Joe: He's a lovable pain in the butt.

Me: So, what did you think when you first met him? Go on, you can be as brutally honest as you like.

Joe: I guess I was probably a bit taken aback. I'd never really met any children with autism before so I was a bit unsure what to expect. He'd only really briefly come downstairs so it was hard to get an opinion straight away.

Me: What is it like to be a stepdad?

Joe: Umm, nice. It's really good, quite fulfilling. I guess it's a different feeling to being a father. It's more like friends and then you get closer as time goes on. So, getting to know them. You don't have that natural bond so it takes time but it's a learning curve. But it's insightful and fun to learn different things about the kids. I appreciate the fact that they look up to me as a dad type figure so that's nice.

Me: I have to say from my viewpoint, I adore watching your relationship with Elsa. You two are so close and I know she sees you as a dad.

Joe: It's pretty amazing to have someone else's child to look up to you and see you as her father. It's quite a responsibility but wonderful that she dotes on me and wants to share things with me as a dad would do, go riding on our bikes and having fun like that. So, it's been good practice for when we had Emmeline. It wasn't such a shock when we had our own child because I kind of knew what to expect. Elsa can be infuriating but that's just kids and they can't control their emotions at times. She's a great kid though and I love her to bits.

Me: What do you see Jude doing as a teenager? I mean in terms of friends, groups, etc.

Joe: I don't know. It depends on how he develops, doesn't it? He's only going to mix with similar minded people; it would be difficult for typical teenagers to be able to build that friendship. I guess he could hang out with children much younger. His communication is the thing that would hold him back, you know, holding a conversation and he gets distracted so quickly so building friendships would be more difficult for him. But he's happy on his own a lot of the time so is always able to entertain himself and he doesn't know any different so it's not like he's missing out on anything. He's in the world of Jude.

Me: And more long term?

Joe: I can imagine him working somewhere like volunteering where there's maybe no stress. I don't know; it depends on how his schooling goes and how he responds. Maybe something that he's good at will come out and he can specialise but like you say, you don't know how he's going to develop. You just hope he can find a place to fulfil his mind and fill his days. It's hard to know, he may be twenty but still have the mind of a four-year-old or he could have a great teenage experience and really develop.

And as a finale... Here's Jude. I wanted to include him directly in this some way so thought I'd interview him to get his thoughts and suggestions on the topic of himself! I asked him each question about four times as his answers were always very short.

Me: Jude. How are you today?
Jude: Good. I'm good today.
Me: How are you enjoying school?
Jude: Yes (I asked what he liked at school next): I like having snacks at school and playing. I like doing my morning work (he has set tasks for the morning before he's allowed play time).
Me: What do you like to do outside of school? Like at the weekend?
Jude: I like going to the park, swimming, that's all. I like seeing Granny. I like playing in my room.
Me: Do you like having two sisters?
Jude: Yes, I like to play. Elsa is ignoring me.
Me: What makes you laugh?
Jude: Jude makes me laugh.(!) I like being happy, being happy makes me laugh.
Me: Does anything make you sad?
Jude: Crying. No snacks.
Me: Jude, are you happy? I hope so because we all love you.
Jude: Yes, I'm happy. Friends make me happy. Playing outside at school and in the garden.

Well, take from that what you want! I think it highlights the wonderful randomness of the boy we call Jude.

If you have enjoyed this book then please follow my blog for more day-to-day experiences of Jude and our family – find us at www.livingwithajude.co.uk

Please let me know your thoughts on my writing; it would mean so much to get your feedback.

Thank you :)

As with everything in a child's life, the pace of experience moves at an astonishing rate. So here we have:

A YEAR ON...

Jude finally had his autism assessment in April 2017 and it was quite blatantly obvious that he is as autistic as you can be. During the assessment, I chatted to a Paediatrician whilst Jude was in a room playing games (naturally set up for them to observe certain, if apparent, characteristics) and then we had a conversation all together once they had conferred over lunch. They were all really lovely and the entire situation lasted no more than a few hours. It was funny because I wasn't set up for anything other than them telling me what I had already deduced so when I heard the words "Jude definitely presents on the spectrum" I rather stupidly yet instinctively replied, "yes, I know."

Another interesting revelation at this meeting is that the Paediatrician isn't entirely convinced of Jude's microcephaly. Yes, she agrees his head circumference is on the low side however she doesn't believe he displays the typical attributes of a microcephalic child. I'm yet to receive her report so it will be interesting what she concludes. This piece of information shocked me a little. Not because I disagree with her, merely because for the last eleven years this has been Jude's primary diagnosis. Our staple answer when people ask what is "wrong" with Jude. It's always been a part of Jude and whilst I don't adhere to the theory of a disability making a person, it certain has formed many elements of his beliefs, his behaviours, his mannerisms and his overall being. He's Jude. He has microcephaly. Or so I thought. Now he's Jude. "Yes, he does have autism." This is possibly my most asked question by absolute strangers - is he autistic? Now, at least I have a resolute answer!

I came away from our assessment meeting feeling so positive. I finally have a viable diagnosis that means we can move forward and find Jude the education and long-term support he really needs.

This leads onto another biggy in terms of change and one I can only advise you of in limited detail because the situation is still on-going. Recently, Jude moved to a local special needs secondary school. It's one I have always admired and hoped Jude could attend as the grounds are beautiful, the school itself is well run, well respected and the children always seem happy. To begin with a positive, I'm incredibly proud of how Jude has taken so well to going to school on a new bus with a new driver, new escort, new bunch of children. The journey to school has always caused Jude a great deal of anxiety, especially the wait for the arrival of the bus as we can't predict exactly when it will turn up and this alone sometimes sends Jude over the edge. I think the great role models on board are helping with all of this initial anxiety which is what I was hoping for across the board with this new transition. However, it was a mere two days into the settling in period when I felt that something wasn't quite right. I had, what I believe was maternal instinct that this was all a big mistake and actually, this school really isn't the one for Jude. People have told me to give it a chance and that he'll get used to it but I just know this isn't true. Jude doesn't get used to things like most people, he either likes them and flourishes or he hates them and it gradually gets worse. And anyway, I don't want him to just get used to something, I want it to be the setting that will help educate Jude and form him into a respectable, independent and well rounded grown up. I don't want him to just get through each day unscathed. The problem is that this school is quite academic (in relative terms) and I get the impression Jude feels intimidated and very much overwhelmed. When he doesn't fit in somewhere and there is an immediate realisation of this fact, Jude's response is traditionally to sabotage the entire situation. It's like he knows he isn't as clever as people in his class so he does what he can to get attention and that means playing up, being sent home and getting back into his comfort zone. And the fact that the school have already excluded Jude from a couple of activities shows me that they feel the same as I do. I'm so sad because I don't sense they have put a huge amount of effort in. I'm not sure what they were expecting of him, especially as they visited him prior to transferring from his old school so should appreciate his capabilities.

Immediately after I realised what a huge error I had made, I arranged to call the school I really wanted him to attend in the first place which is entirely for children on the autistic spectrum; I'm going to visit this week. I was not allowed to visit previously as no relevant diagnosis had been given - this was another reason for my happiness at the assessment outcome. The next thing I did was call a meeting with all professionals currently involved in Jude's social and educational care and this is being held very soon. I called this meeting with the primary aim of naming an alternative school that I would like Jude to attend and as long as his current Headteacher is in agreement that they cannot meet his needs (and I believe very strongly that they will be in agreement with me) then he should be able to move. Oh, it all sounds so simple but you just know it won't be so!

Following the above, I should tell you about the professionals now regularly involved in Jude's care. In a nutshell, we have an SEN Officer who is in charge of Jude's educational requirements and we have a Social Worker who is in charge of Jude's and the rest of the families needs at home. It took me a very long time to get to where we are now and it certainly involved a great deal of tears and tantrums on my part. I got to a very dark stage where I felt I was about to have a break down but thankfully, our (now) Social Worker agreed to visit me at home to ascertain what we really need as a whole family. We were offered additional Support Worker hours which we still have in place but I've struggled to find anyone to fill the position and actually, I'm not sure I find this level of support particularly helpful. He sees one lady for four hours every fortnight and this is fantastic, she is amazing with him and he really enjoys himself; it means Joe and I can take the girls out for a little while and have a break and we certainly return home refreshed and ready for the rest of our Sunday. I have explained to my Social Worker that the only way I could find those additional hours in any way conducive was if we could find someone to help out in the mornings before school and at bedtime for an hour or so but realistically, who would want a job with such random hours? I have advertised for the space however, so far the only applicants have been very specific about where they could include the hours in their week and it just doesn't fit with us to be so exacting. I find the experience of someone entering our house and unequivocally taking over from me as figurehead in one of my children's lives a very strange emotion. I know that's a bit of a dramatic statement but handing over the reins of responsibility at half passed nine every other Sunday is almost tangible in the case of Jude, there's no gliding transition, it's a solid lump of a "here's what you need to know" scenario." In an ideal world I would like Jude to attend a weekly boarding school however, I have been told by the council that I will have a fight on my hands for this (what they consider) enormous request. I replied that through my research, children like Jude who attend boarding school very often come out the other end more confident, self-assured, independent and with the ability to use their own initiative. Jude has none of these skills right now and I'm afraid of him turning eighteen one day and not even being able to know what he has planned for the day or where he should be at what time. It would be amazing for him to have the education that is BEST for him, yet the council consider budgets more important than ideal scenarios. I know he won't have a glowing career but I want what will make him the best Jude he can be. To tell me I will have to fight for what is best for my son is horrendous. This is the Social CARE department yet I have experienced very little care of which I haven't had to beg for.

I wasn't going to publish this but I have been told that it really exudes emotion that no-one can truly comprehend unless they have been in our situation. Before reading it, I want you to know that this isn't a criticism of solely our council. It goes way higher than this, to the government who, I believe, truly care not one jot about the vulnerable and disabled in our society. Our county council are given a budget and I appreciate that they have to spread it as well as they possibly can. My irk is with our entire system as a nation that shies away from responsibilities and hides away the true realities of those in need.

Dear HCC,

Please excuse the ubiquitous letter however so many people and so many departments have factored into our time in Hertfordshire that I can't particularly address it to one individual. That would be unfair and unrealistic.

I have had quite an emotional week with one thing or another but what has pretty much tipped me over the edge in terms of how I feel is the inability of you, HCC to make my life that little bit simpler. Not just my life, my son Jude's life. It's a silly little thing really, just a school transfer. We have been waiting for a date since the summer and between August when Jude was initially offered the chance of an early transfer to a school I have always wanted him to attend and now, I have probably spoken to around thirty people, all of whom have attempted to transfer me onto another department/ team/individual. Only today (15th November 2016), after all these months have I finally located the person in charge of our "case". A case. My son's educational and social needs are lumped under that rather arduous and indeterminable word void of any personable or thoughtful meaning.

The inexplicable enormity of this one silly little issue of a date for my sons transfer has brought back a wave of bad memories relating to the constant battle I have had with you to ensure my son receives the therapy and care he needs, the care that only professionals and specialists can provide. Specialists such as Physiotherapists, Occupational Therapists, Speech Therapists and Music Therapists, all of whom he was refused access to which was strange because in our previous county Jude had received all of the above, without question or issue on a weekly basis. All of which he was refused despite the fact they were mentioned as beneficial and in some cases necessary within his (then) Statement of Educational Need.

I feel like you have most ardently failed me in my role as a mother. I appreciate that responsibility for Jude ultimately falls on my shoulders however without support, I can only do so much. Let's focus on what I consider the main two professional areas necessary for my son:

Firstly, Physiotherapy. Jude had an assessment when he was about five however, it was deemed impossible to offer him any sessions because he could already walk. Yes, walk. The benchmark for being physically ay-ok by HCC is the ability to successfully get from Point A to Point B on your feet. Needless to say this denial was refuted however, it is evidently a pointless fight. I actually had a row with one of the "main" Physiotherapy team members because she felt I was unreasonable insisting on Jude having this type of support. How dare I expect more than a basic movement for my son! At the age of now almost eleven he cannot even climb a climbing frame and prefers to hold onto a buggy or take a hand when walking through town as he is still very wobbly.

Occupational Therapy – Jude was refused this on the grounds that his concentration was not good enough which is a pretty harsh judgement for a five year old child with learning disabilities. This is one area in which I feel I have failed Jude the most. At his current stage, he is still unable to do up a zip, button up his coat or put his shoes on himself. He can hold a pencil and write his name fairly legibly but his finger strength is incredibly weak. Yes, I know I could do a lot more to help these notably standard activities however attempting to fit Occupational Therapy sessions into an already busy household is unrealistic. The Occupational Therapist we used to see in our previous county used to give Jude weekly exercises and it is this spoon feeding of information and guidance that a mother like me needs. She used to also claim how great a focused session was for Jude's concentration as sitting and working on an activity does not come naturally to Jude; it really made a difference but you didn't listen.

Because of the trillions of phone calls I have had to chase up, the referrals we have waited patiently for, the paperwork I've ploughed through, the transferring through your complex web of telephone centres, the hospital assessments, the let downs and the baffling amount of people I have to speak to just to find out when my son will be moving schools, I feel emotionally broken. I feel I have failed my son and I blame you largely for this sensitivity. I now have this overwhelming guilt and anxiety that I could have done better. Why couldn't I have just listed down all the people involved in one assessment, why didn't I jot down this number or that number because now we have to start again and I've wasted another week calling back and forth, why didn't I fight the refusal for this or that therapy, why didn't I ask around for contacts and possible support networks?! Largely because I was lost and looking for your social care department to guide me but this never happened.

When we moved to Hertfordshire it was literally a few months before Jude was starting school. I assumed, with his Statement of Educational Need making reference to his SEVERE learning disabilities, his need for someone with him to change his pull ups and all the other problems he then faced that we would be given the option of a special needs (SEN) school. I even visited a few and chose my favourite however, whilst on the phone to…I have no idea because I spoke to so many different people…I was told that there was no way we could have a SEN school because Jude was "not known" to the system. I thought that was why he had a Statement. I argued my case however, because of the short time frame I was told to choose a mainstream school there and then on the phone. Luckily, I know the area so chose what I felt was best however, is that really a way to treat a mother trying to find the best provision for her disabled son? I was told I could take it to panel however this is a long process and Jude would lose any mainstream place in the meantime. I was basically backed into a corner and as such, Jude spent his reception year feeling inadequate amongst his peers and barely involving himself in class activities. I spent a year feeling awkward in the playground at pick up and drop off time. The teaching team spent a year attempting to involve Jude in group class work knowing it was entirely futile because he had no idea what they were on about. We were lucky he had fantastic Learning

Support Assistants however, again these were only part funded by you despite the fact Jude was incredibly vulnerable, unable to sit in class and still in pull ups. You thought it was ok for him to spend an entire afternoon each day unsupported but thankfully his school thought otherwise and financed his carer partly themselves.

Anyway, I could write a letter a hundred pages long – in the ten and a half years Jude has been alive, he has spent over half of these in Hertfordshire so we have many tales to tell. However, I will leave it at this for now. I just wanted to let you know, HCC, that you have failed me as a mother and as such you have failed my family and in particular my son, Jude.

I just wonder how confident, fantastic, articulate, outgoing, popular, social, fun and most importantly happy Jude would be if things had been different.

Yours sincerely,

Alice Soule

So following this letter, we were offered a physio and occupational therapy assessment however, I did something really stupid and muddled up my days. On attempting to re-book our session, it was suggested to me that we wait whilst Jude settles into his new school and it was explained how great their abilities are within this school so external physio and OT may not be necessary. I agreed to see how it goes but now this has pretty much all blown up in the air, we may be back at square one until I find access to an adequate school for Jude.

It continues…

So what of Jude's weirdies? Well, he's still phobic of glasses and the number of pairs I have lost over the last year is pretty extravagant. Funnily enough, I found a stash of them shoved down the back of one of the kitchen drawers this week so I managed to hook them out with a coat hanger! It's so funny, I wonder what he sees in a pair of glasses!

Jude no longer plays with building blocks in bed but instead, he rips up lots and lots of paper and flicks them around his pillow whilst he lies down. I think it's something to do with the motion in front of his eyes, similar to when he's watching television; observing just below the image so he can see the colours moving around above his eye line. It's quite remarkable and I truly hope that one day Jude can explain what he sees in his paper flicking and television watching! He doesn't have any other new weirdies, I don't think. Oh maybe one which is again when we're in the car - he absolutely hates it if I turn the radio off and insists the music is brought back on; he loves music, it's always been a real passion for Jude.

One really fun (read: insane, potentially catastrophic) thing we did with Jude and the girls recently was to go glamping. I'm not a camper in any way whatsoever, but the thought of a tent that is more like a house certainly appealed to my outdoorsy side. It was really good fun and certainly expanded Jude's horizons on his own little levels. Occasionally, he preferred to stay in the tent where he felt safe and other times he ventured out with us into the woods to play with the tree swing and explore our surroundings. I think my favourite visual memory so far this year is displayed in this photo. I absolutely love it. Doesn't it make you smile? What a bunch we have! I wanted to leave you on a happy note and I think this image sums up the crazy three perfectly.

But finally... I'm convinced Jude is about to hit puberty and again, this scares the life out of me! A friend of mine has a son a few years older than Jude but of a similar level of disability and she said it can be somewhat challenging at times because he has no idea what is going on and she can't explain to him why he feels certain ways. As if adolescence isn't traumatic enough. How will it change Jude? What situations are we going to find ourselves in over the next few years? I'm pretty excited to see Jude growing up so fast and I'm adoring having a child of his age but with a child like Jude comes that realisation that he will never truly grow up. I'll let you know how we get on in the next chapter of living with a Jude.